Jane's Dog Guide
to
San Diego

by
Frank Stollenwerk
&
Paul Burke

Jane's Dog Guide
to
San Diego

To place orders, send in the order form at the back of this book or fax orders to (619)280-7699, (619)280-7596 fax or visit our website at *www.janesdogguide.com*.

Information in this book was researched and edited. All rates, directions and information are accurate at the time of this printing but may subsequently change. *Jane's Dog Guide's*, Frank Stollenwerk and Paul Burke are not responsible for any discrepancies or changes.

Contact us at www.janesdogguide.com to have your dog-friendly business, organization or favorite dog place added to the next edition of *Jane's Dog Guide to San Diego*.

Library of Congress Catalog Card Number: SF 427.4574.C2 58 2001

Published in 2001 by Jane's Dog Guide.

No agency or establishment listed in this book have contributed money to this project.

ISBN 0-9712726-0-3
Printed in the United States of America

Dedicated to:
Fluffy

To my beloved Fluffy, the best little dog in the world and to all homeless dogs wandering aimlessly in the streets in search of a loving home.

Acknowledgments

Writing this book has been a long, yet enjoyable journey and we could not have done it alone. There are many people that have contributed and we hope that everyone realizes how much we appreciate their help, insights and support.

We would like to give special thanks to Casey Orr, who gave us countless hours of her time to take many of the photographs for the book. Her love for dogs and photography is an amazing combination that shines through her work. Assisting Casey, and taking care of Jane during some of the photo shoots, was Jerrale Morris, whose love for animals and people made him a valuable asset.

Special thanks go to Donald Burke and Michelle Hawkins for data checking and editing, Katherine LePage for the logo design, Angie Roberts of Graphic Details for layout, typography and cover design and Ann Silberman for writing.

Many thanks go to Beverly Barr, whose time spent at the coffee shop from the early stages to present kept the motivation going during some dry periods. Also, thanks to Carol Frederick and Jeannette Kingery, both huge motivators and supporters of *Jane's Dog Guide.*

And of course, loving thanks to our moms, Joan Goehring and Wally Stollenwerk, whose love and affection through the years have provided the drive to complete this project.

Paul Burke
Frank Stollenwerk

Introduction

Dogs have been faithful companions to humans throughout the ages. As a species, we have long relied on dogs, not only for company, but also for important work. They lead the blind, comfort the sick, and find the lost. They work endlessly and contentedly in the service of man.

Of course, their special gift is that they provide companionship in its purest form. Dogs offer love without secrets, cheerfulness without demands, obedience for the asking, and joy without artifice.

It is a sad fact that in today's society we are becoming increasingly isolated from other people. Neighbors don't know one another. Family may be far away, and friends are scattered throughout the world. We work and play on the computer; we often have solitary jobs that create a feeling of loneliness and separation from other humans. We stay inside our homes and watch television, sometimes with dogs as our only friends.

And yet, something exciting is starting to happen. Out of this isolation a new kinship is forming. Slowly, dogs are bringing humans together, forming a new type of community.

This new community consists of people who love their dogs and recognize their value. Dog enthusiasts are starting to gather together in appreciation of the joys that dogs can bring. Businesses are recognizing this community and are beginning to cater to it. Coffee shops are creating dog-friendly spaces, as are hotels and restaurants. Dog parks are opening, and traveling with our animal companions is becoming the norm.

Out of this new dog culture, *Jane's Dog Guide* was born. *Jane's Dog Guide* is a book dedicated to putting San Diego folks together with their dogs in places where they're wanted and accepted.

Within this book you will find not only San Diego community resources for dog lovers, but also photographs, personal experiences of those who live here, and observations of responsible and loving dog relationships. In addition, *Jane's Dog Guide* will touch on the cruelty of haphazard and thoughtless breeding of animals.

Why is this book called *Jane's Dog Guide*? Jane is our dog, a Briard-Chow mix we rescued from the streets of Tijuana. This book was born out of our love of Jane and the guidance Jane has given us. Jane has allowed us a strong understanding of the dog community, as well as opened up new places to have fun with our animal companions. We want to share those experiences with others in our region.

Join Jane, and us, as we guide you through the friendly and active world of the San Diego dog community. Together we'll explore all there is to do in this rich and beautiful part of the world.

How to Use This Book

The chapters in this book all include an introduction to that particular chapter. It tells you what the chapter is all about and what you can find in the following pages.

The proceeding pages within the chapter will be split into halves.

> The interior halves will alphabetically list all the resources and places to take your dog by city. This symbol (✱) denotes that the place is leash-free. You will find this symbol in the beach and parks chapters.
>
> The exterior halves will provide photos of dogs in and around San Diego County. They show the diverse types of dogs within our dog community.

You will also read many tips that we, or someone in our community, have provided.

These symbols will denote the following:

 General tips

 Grooming tips

 Money saving tips

 Health tips

 Dog etiquette

 Warnings

 Shopping tips

 Training tips

✦ Directions

✱ Leash free location

About the Authors

Frank Stollenwerk is a civil engineer for the City of San Diego and has lived in San Diego for ten years. He became interested in dog-friendly places after encountering a "No Dogs Allowed" sign at his once favorite hiking site outside of Julian.

Paul Burke has worked at the Society for the Prevention of Cruelty to Animals and Veterinary offices and is now a computer consultant in San Diego. He has lived here for twelve years. Paul has always had a love for animals and has rescued many dogs and cats in his life, including Jane.

Table of Contents

Chapter One

Beaches

BEACHES

San Diego is world-renowned for its golden beauty and moderate climate, and its many beaches play no small part in its reputation as a great place to relax. Surrounding San Diego are miles and miles of beautiful coastline, and with our year-round warm weather we have plenty of opportunity to enjoy this natural resource with our pets.

©Casey Orr

San Diego is a very dog-friendly county, and nowhere is this more evident than on our shores. We are lucky to be able to choose between an off-leash or an on-leash beach romp with our pet. On cooler mornings one can take a slow, contented on-leash walk by the sandstone bluffs, just you and your animal companion listening to the sound of the gentle waves.

Other times, you might need a bit more activity, and then an off-leash romp may be in order. There your dog can run free to play in the surf, catch sticks or sniff at the strange animals that come up from the sea.

Exploring a beach can really be an adventure for your pooch. Dogs need to play with you to be truly happy, and there is no more perfect place to play than a wide, sandy beach with lots of room to run. In this next chapter, Jane will guide you through the world of San Diego's beaches.

We will let you know which beaches allow pets on leashes and which will allow your animal companion to roam free. We will also be providing you with tips to care for your sandy pet after a romp and may share a product or tip on keeping your car sand-free. You will also find other general information that will be useful to you as you and your dog begin to discover San Diego's gorgeous beaches.

CARDIFF

Cardiff State Beach

Old Highway 101

✦ Take I-5 to Lomas Santa Fe. Head north on S21 (Old Highway 101) to the south end of Cardiff State Beach across from San Elijo Lagoon. Dogs allowed on leash south of campground near Tower 7.

CHULA VISTA

Bayside Park

End of Bayside Parkway near Chula Vista Harbor

✦ Take I-5 to Marina Parkway/J Street Exit. Head west on Marina Parkway. Turn west on Sandpiper Way. Turn onto Bayside Parkway and take to the end.

CORONADO

Coronado City Dog Beach ✱

Ocean Boulevard South of Naval Base

✦ Take I-5 to 75 West over the Coronado Bridge. Turn west onto Orange Avenue. Turn north onto Ocean Boulevard and take all the way to the Naval Base. Leash-free.

Coronado Tidelands Regional Park

Mullinix Drive

✦ Take I-5 to 75 West over the Coronado Bridge. Turn left onto Glorietta Boulevard. Make another left onto Mullinix Drive to parking lot.

DEL MAR

Del Mar Beach

6th to 17th Street

✦ Take I-5 to Del Mar Heights Road. Go straight to 4th Avenue and head north onto Stratford Court. Park between 6th and 17th Streets. Leashes required.

In light of recent water pollution attributed to doggy waste, its critically important that you pick up after your dog. We love our leash-free beaches and want to keep them forever. Aside from it being part of responsible pet ownership, violators can be fined up to $250.

Jane says, "Watch out for these things while at the beach:

- *Sting rays*
- *Jellyfish*
- *Sharp objects*
- *Hot coals"*

©Casey Orr

Doggie paws are very sensitive and can cut easily, stung and even burn on hot sand.

©Casey Orr

Always bring fresh water with you when going to the beach. Dogs overheat easily and may drink the salt water if thirsty. Salt water can make your dog sick.

Del Mar Rivermouth Dog Beach ✪
Near 29th Street
✦ Take I-5 to Valle de la Via. Head west to S21 (Camino del Mar) and turn south. Leash-free from September 15 to June 15. Leashes required during summer months.

ENCINITAS

San Elijo State Beach
S21 (Old Highway 101) and Chesterfield Drive
✦ Take I-5 to Birmingham Drive west. Turn south onto San Elijo Avenue. Turn west at Chesterfield Drive.

SAN DIEGO

Fiesta Island ✪
Fiesta Island Road
✦ Take I-5 to Sea World Drive. Head West to Mission Bay Drive. Turn north onto Mission Bay Drive. Turn west onto Fiesta Island Road. The whole island is leash-free.

La Jolla Shores Beach
La Verda Paseo & Vallecitos Court at Kellogg Park
✦ Take I-5 to Ardath Road west. Take Torrey Pines Road west to La Jolla Shores Drive north. Turn west on Vallecitos and take to the end. Dogs allowed from 6pm to 9am. Leashes required.

Mission Bay Park
Mission Bay Drive at De Anza Cove
✦ Take I-5 to Mission Bay Drive/Clairemont Drive exit. Head west to Visitor Information Center. Turn north onto Mission Bay Drive to De Anza Road. Dogs allowed from 6pm to 9am. Leashes required.

Mission Beach/Pacific Beach
Mission Boulevard to Mission Bay Drive
✦ Take I-5 to Garnet Avenue. Head west to Mission Boulevard. 3 miles long. Dogs allowed from 6pm to 9am on beach and boardwalk. Leashes required.

Ocean Beach Dog Beach ✪
W. Point Loma Boulevard and Voltaire Street
✦ Take I-8 to Sunset Cliffs Boulevard west. Turn west onto W. Point Loma Boulevard to Voltaire Street. Leash-free.

Ocean Beach Park
South of Ocean Beach Dog Beach at W. Point Loma Boulevard
✦ Take I-8 to Sunset Cliffs Boulevard west. Turn west onto W. Point Loma Boulevard to Voltaire Street . 0.5 miles long. Dogs allowed between 6pm to 9am. Leashes required.

Point La Jolla Beaches
Coast Boulevard at La Jolla Cove
✦ Take I-5 to Ardath Road west. Take Torrey Pines Road west and turn west on Prospect Road. Turn west onto Coast Boulevard to La Jolla Cove. Dogs allowed from 6pm to 9am on beach and trails. Leashes required.

"Don't worry about fleas at the beach. Salt water kills them and they can't live on dry sand. And there is no such thing as sand fleas in San Diego. So, don't be afraid to bring your dog to the beach."

Jane Donley
Dog Beach Dog Wash
Breaker, Mattie and Dash, randomly mixed-breed rescues
Ocean Beach

©Casey Orr

NOTES

Chapter Two

Parks

Parks

©Casey Orr

If San Diego's beaches are the jewels of the county, then the park system must be its golden setting. The parks of San Diego are lush and beautiful, filled with diverse plant life and a variety of landscapes. On any given day one can choose a peaceful stroll around a small community park filled with friendly people, or decide to delve into a wilderness complete with canyon trails. Within only a few miles you and your pet can explore a backwoods setting or relax at a manicured park where flowers are abundant and eucalyptus and palm trees bloom side-by-side.

Taking your dog to a regional San Diego park just may be the definitive Southern California experience. In the warm sunshine, among the displays of seasonal flowers, dogs and dog-lovers come together to play ball, walk along the shady paths, and get to know each other. One sees in-line skaters taking their dogs for a run, or passes kids throwing sticks to their beloved pets.

Especially in the off-leash parks, friendliness is the custom and a sense of community is easily fostered. All who are there are united in their desire to exercise their dogs and have fun doing it. Because of this common interest, these parks are wonderful gathering places for dog-owners to meet and mingle. The pleasing surroundings are perfect for opening up to your fellow dog-lovers. In doing so, one gains a sense of kinship and appreciation for the rich ethnic diversity of the community. Of course, the parks are also a great place for your dog to have fun and get that all-important exercise and fresh air, as well as an excellent place for them to learn to socialize with others.

In this next chapter, we will explore all that the parks in San Diego have to offer. Of course, we'll share the locations of the best on and off-leash parks, but we'll also emphasize the joys of exercising with your pet and the benefits of healthy socialization. San Diego's parks have much to offer both you and your dog and are rich in activities you can share, not only with your dog, but with the rest of your community.

ALPINE

Flinns Spring Regional Park
14800 Old Highway 80

Lake Jennings Regional Park
End of Bass Drive off Lake Jennings Park Road

CHULA VISTA

Bayside Park
End of Bayside Parkway at Chula Vista Harbor

Palomar Park
Park Drive off E. Palomar Street

CORONADO

Centennial Park
Orange Avenue and First Street near the Old Ferry Landing

Coronado Cays Park
Coronado Cays Boulevard at Grand Caribe Causeway off of Silver Strand Boulevard

Coronado Tidelands Regional Park
Mullinix Drive off Glorietta Boulevard

EL CAJON AREA

Damon Lane County Park
Damon Lane and Zoldero Road

Deputy Lonnie G. Brewer County Park
10000 Fury Lane off Avocado Boulevard

Cottonwood County Park
Hilton Head Road & Muirfield Drive off of Willow Glen Drive

Nancy Jane County Park
La Cresta Boulevard & Lilac Drive

The City of San Diego Park Ordinances for all parks, other than designated leash-free dog parks:

- *You must keep your dog on a leash no greater than 8 feet long at all times.*
- *Your dog must be legally licensed and wear a registration tag.*
- *You must clean up after your own dog, so come prepared with bags.*
- *No dogs are allowed on any athletic field at any time.*
- *You must accept full responsibility and liability for your dog's actions.*

©Casey Orr

Tie plastic grocery bags onto your dog's leash and keep some extra ones in your glove compartment in your car. They can be used for doggie poopie bags. Replace them as soon as you use them so you are never left holding without a bag.

ENCINITAS

Encinitas Viewpoint Park
Cornish Drive & D Street

Orpheus Park
482 Orpheus Avenue at Union Street

ESCONDIDO

Elfin Forest Recreational Reserve
9900 Harmony Grove Road

E. Escondido Dog Park ✪
E. Valley Parkway (S6) near Lake Wohlford Road

Felicita Regional Park
742 Clarence Lane off Felicita Road

FALLBROOK

Fallbrook Community Park
Fallbrook Street (S15) & Heald Lane

Live Oak Regional Park
Reche Road (S15) & Grid Road

IMPERIAL BEACH

Imperial Beach Sports Park
5th & Imperial Beach Boulevard

Tijuana River National Estuarine Sanctuary
300 Caspian Way & 3rd Street off Imperial Beach Boulevard

LA MESA AREA

Eucalyptus County Park
Edgewood Drive & Bancroft Drive

Harry Griffin Park
Janfred Way & Milden Street off Water Street
Lake Murray
End of Kiowa Drive off Lake Murray Boulevard

NATIONAL CITY

Lincoln Acres County Park
2717 Granger Avenue at Chaffee Street

OCEANSIDE

Buddy Todd Memorial Park
3000 Mesa Drive & Parnassus Circle

Guajome Regional Park
Guajome Lake Road off Mission Avenue

POWAY

Blue Sky Ecological Preserve Hike
Espola Road (S5) & Green Valley Trucktrial

Iron Mountain Trail Hike
Poway Road & Highway 67

Lake Poway Recreational Area
End of Lake Poway Road off Espola Road

Poway Community Dog Park ✪
Bowrun Rd & Creek Park Drive off Poway Rd
Leash free dawn to dusk

RAMONA

Collier County Park
7th Street & 'E' Street

SAN DIEGO

Allied Gardens Community Park
5155 Greenbrier Avenue
Allied Gardens

Balboa Park ✪
Balboa Drive at El Prado

Bay View Park & Dog Park
Felspar Street and Soledad Mountain Road
Pacific Beach

Black Mountain Open Space
Black Mountain Road off Ted Williams Freeway (56)
Rancho Penasquitos

©Casey Orr

The City of San Diego is considering building 5 new leash-free dog parks including:

- *Capehart area in Pacific Beach*
- *Camino Ruiz at Calle Cristobal in Mira Mesa*
- *Nobel Athletic area in University City*
- *North Chollas Park in Oak Park*
- *Sandburg Park in Mira Mesa.*

Unfortunately, there is opposition to this proposition, so Jane says, bark out loud and contact your Council member.

"The Iams Corporation is partnering with the City of San Diego by purchasing and installing 34 mutt mitt dispensers for various parks around the city. The City believes that the mutt mitts will further encourage pet owners to pick up pet waste and keep City parks clean for all park users."

Covering Ground Newsletter

©Casey Orr

Cadman Community Park ✱
Wayne Lane & Avati Drive
Clairemont
Leash free 7:30-10:00am & 4:40-7:00pm

Canyonside Community Park
12350 Black Mountain Road at Truman St.
Mira Mesa

Chollas Lake Park
6350 College Grove Drive
Oak Park

City Heights Recreation Center
3777 44th Street
City Heights

Clairemont Community Park
3500 block Clairemont Drive
Clairemont

Ellen Browning Scripps Park
1180 Coast Boulevard at Ocean Lane
La Jolla

Embarcadero Marina Park
Kettner Boulevard at Seaport Village
Port District Downtown

Encanto Community Park
6508 Wunderlin Avenue at 65th Street
North Encanto

Golden Hill Community Park
2600 Golf Course Drive off 26th Street
Golden Hill

Grape Street Dog Park ✱
2800 Grape Street near Granada Avenue
Golden Hill
Leash free: M-F 7:30-10:00am & 4-9:00pm
Sat/Sun/Holiday 9-11:00am & 4-9:00pm

Harbor Island Drive Park
Harbor Island Drive off Harbor Drive
Harbor Island

Kate O. Sessions Park
5115 Soledad Road at Park Drive
Pacific Beach

Kearny Mesa Community Park
3170 Armstrong Street at Mesa College Drive
Kearny Mesa

Kellogg Park
Camino Del Oro at Vallecitos
La Jolla Shores

Linda Vista Community Park
7064 Levant Street off Fulton Street
Linda Vista

Maddox Park ✱
Flanders Drive and Dabney Drive
Mira Mesa

Marion Bear Memorial Park
Soledad Freeway (52) & Regents Road or Genessee Avenue
Clairemont

Mira Mesa Community Park
8575 New Salem Street off Mira Mesa Boulevard
Mira Mesa

Mission Trails Regional Park
8102 Father Juniper Serra Trail off Mission Gorge Drive
Tierrasanta

Morley Field Dog Park ✱
Morley Field Drive & Jacaranda Place
Balboa Park

Mount Soledad Natural Park
Soledad Road off Via Capri
Mount Soledad

Nates Point ✱
El Prado & Balboa Dr. (near 6th & Laurel)
Balboa Park

©Casey Orr

Poway's Dog Park was founded in 1996 by Bob Burkhardt, a Poway resident and dog trainer. For more information on Poway's Dog Park and its history, check out: www.ci.poway.ca.us/dogpark/history.htm.

©Casey Orr

Be adventurous . . . drive to a new neighborhood and explore other community parks with your dog.

North Park Community Park
4044 Idaho Street between Howard and Lincoln Avenues
North Park

Paradise Hills Community Park & Recreation Center
6610 Potomac Street
Paradise Hills

Quivira Basin
2581 Quivira Court off Quivira Way
Mission Bay Park

Rose Canyon Open Space
7900 block Genesee Avenue
University Avenue

Serra Mesa Community Park
9020 Village Glen Drive off Ruffin Road
Serra Mesa

Spanish Landing Park
4500 block North Harbor Drive
Harbor Island

Standley Community Park
3585 Governor Drive & Mercer Street
University City

Tecolote Canyon Natural Park
Tecolote Road off Morena Boulevard
Clairemont

Tierrasanta Community Park
11220 Clairemont Mesa Boulevard
Tierrasanta

SPRING VALLEY

Goodland Acres County Park
8800 block Troy Street

Spring Valley Park
8900 block Jamacha Boulevard at Gillespie Drive

SWEETWATER

Sweetwater County Park
3218 Summit Meadow

VISTA

Buena Vista Park
Melrose Drive & Shadowridge Drive

"Always have your dog collared and tagged in case he or she wanders off. There are many canyons around the San Diego leash free area and dogs are VERY curious about them."

Rich
Eldin - Husky/Pyrenees Mix
Southpark

©*Casey Orr*

NOTES

Chapter Three

©Casey Orr

Hiking

Hiking

©Casey Orr

Among all of the activities you and your dog can share, none will give you a sense of San Diego's landscape better than its hiking trails. While visiting beaches and parks will offer you and your dog the opportunity to meet others and have playful experiences, hiking offers unprecedented access to the rugged beauty of areas in the county that not everyone encounters.

San Diego has a surprisingly diverse landscape and the topographical variety offers a wide array of hiking experiences. There are miles of hiking trails in the county's parks and open space preserves. Some hikes may take you over craggy mountains and isolated valleys, while others are as simple as a stroll along a quiet stream. You can hike by the churning Pacific Ocean or choose desert landscapes dotted with cacti and sage.

Whatever type of hike you choose, there is no better way for you and your dog to physically exercise. Dogs love to be outdoors and will show boundless enthusiasm for hiking. A pair of pleading brown eyes on a Saturday morning and you will soon find yourself off to the hiking reserves, boots on and ready for a workout. Contrasting with a park or beach experience where the emphasis is on communing with others, taking a hike with your dog underscores the human-to-dog bond. Alone on the trails, you and your dog will not only explore the beauty of nature, but discover adventure together.

Hiking with your animal companion takes effort and preparation. Of course, water is a must-bring, but do you know what makes a good doggie trail mix? In the next pages, we will not only list the hiking trails, but will also help you prepare for the rigors of wilderness hiking with your dog. We'll list the necessities that you will need to keep your dog happy and safe on the trail. Experiencing nature with your closest companion can be a healthy and enjoyable experience if you remember to take just a few precautions.

ANZA-BORREGO DESERT REGION

Kwaaymii Interpretive Trail

✦ Take I-8 to S1 (Sunrise Highway) north. Take S1 for about 24 miles to the Visitor's Information Center and park. Pick up a free pamphlet.

Kwaaymii Point

✦ Take I-8 to S1 (Sunrise Highway) north. Take S1 for about 29 miles to the Pioneer Mail Picnic
Area and park.

CHULA VISTA

Sweetwater River

5500 block of Bonita Road

✦ Take I-805 to Bonita Road exit. Take Bonita Road to the bridge over the Sweetwater River. Cross bridge and park. Hike east along the golf course and over the hills.

CORONADO

Bayshore Bikeway

Silver Strand Boulevard at Glorietta Bay Park

✦ Take I-5 to Hwy 75 west over the Coronado Bridge. Turn west on Orange Avenue. Orange Avenue turns into Silver Strand Boulevard. Turn east onto Rendova Road and park on Strand Way. Hike south along the Silver Strand bikeway and trails.

ESCONDIDO

Felicita Regional Park

742 Clarence Lane

✦ Take I-15 to Via Rancho Parkway exit. Head east on Via Rancho Parkway and turn north onto Felicita Road. Park at Clarance Lane.
Short hikes.

©Casey Orr

Take a spritzer filled with water with you and your dog when going hiking. When thirsty, spritz the water into the side of your dogs mouth to keep them hydrated. The spritzer easily latches onto your pocket or belt.

"Watch out for these things while hiking with your dog:

- *Rattle snakes*
- *Traffic*
- *Sharp objects such as broken glass*
- *Poison oak that can transfer to humans*
- *Other poisonous plants your dog may want to chew*
- *Burrs and foxtails*
- *Ticks*

It's important to keep your dog on his leash to protect them from these things. Dogs will be dogs and there are noises and wild animals that he may chase or explore and if allowed, he may be in harm's way."

©Casey Orr

FALLBROOK

Live Oak Regional Park
Reche Road/Gird Road
✦ Take I-15 to Mission Road Exit. Turn west. Then turn south onto Old Highway 395. Turn west onto Reche Road (S15). Take Reche Road to Gird Road.
(858) 694-3049

IMPERIAL BEACH

Tijuana River National Estuarine Sanctuary
✦ Take I- 5 to Coronado Avenue west. Coronado Avenue turns into Imperial Beach Boulevard. Take Imperial Beach Boulevard to 3rd Avenue and turn south. Visitor Center is at 3rd Avenue and Caspian Way.

JULIAN

Volcan Mountain Wilderness Preserve
Wynola Road & Farmer Road
✦ Take I-15 to 78 east. Take 78 to 78/79 east to Wynola Road. Head east on Wynola Road to Farmer Road north.

William Heisse Regional Park
Frisius Drive
✦ Take I-15 to 78 east. Take 78 to 78/79 east to Pine Hills Road south. Take Pine Hills Road to Frisius Drive east. Take to the end.

LA MESA

Harry Griffin Park
Milden Street & Janfred Way
✦ Take I-8 to Freeway 125 north. Turn right on Amaya Drive. Turn right on Water Street. Turn left on Milden Street and take it the park at Janfred Way.

Lake Murray
Kiowa Drive
✦ Take I-8 to Lake Murray Road north. Turn north onto Kiowa Drive to the parking lot.

LAKESIDE

El Monte Regional Park
El Monte Road
✦ Take I-8 to Lake Jennings Road north to El Monte Road east. Park is passed Mountain Valley Place .

Lake Jennings Regional Park
End of Bass Drive off Lake Jennings Park Rd.
✦ Take I-8 to Lake Jennings Park Road/Olde Highway 80 exit. Take Lake Jennings Park Road north to Bass Drive. Take Bass Drive to the end of the park.

Lindo Lake County Park
Lindo Lane
✦ Take I-8 to Los Coches Road north. Take Los Coches Road to Julian Avenue east. Take Julian Avenue to Caraway north and turn west onto Lindo Lane.

Louis A. Stelzer Regional Park
Wildcat Canyon Road
✦ Take I-8 to 67 north. Take 67 to Mapleview Street east. Turn north onto Ashwood Street. Ashwood Street turns into Wildcat Canyon Road.

MOUNT LAGUNA

Sunset Trail Loop (Cleveland National Forest)
Off Sunrise Highway (S1)
✦ Take I-8 to Sunrise Highway (S1) exit. Take Sunrise Highway north for approximately 19 miles until you see the Meadows Information Station.

OCEANSIDE

Buddy Todd Memorial Park
Mesa Drive & Parnassus Circle
✦ Take I-5 to Mission Avenue east. Take Mission Avenue to Mesa Drive south. Take Mesa Drive to Parnassus Circle.

©Casey Orr

"Be sure to check between your dog's pads for any foreign objects such as foxtails, burrs or small rocks after walking on trails. If present, use tweezers to remove and apply topical antibiotic (Neosporin) to avoid infection."

Sheila Bose
Scout and Tucker
Point Loma

©Casey Orr

"Always pack a first aid kit for you and your dog when going out on long hikes. You never know what accidents may happen while temporarily escaping from civilization."

Michelle Forte
Cookie - German Shepherd
San Diego

Guajome Regional Park
Guajome Lake Road
✦ Take I-5 to SR76 (Mission Avenue) east. Take SR76 to Guajome Lake Road.

PALOMAR MOUNTAIN

Observatory Trail
South Grade Road
✦ Take I-15 to SR76 east. Take SR76 to South Grade Road north. Turn north onto Canfield Road to the Observatory.

POWAY

Blue Sky Ecological Preserve Hike
Espola Road & Green Valley Trucktrail
✦ Take I-15 to Espola Road (S5) east. Take Espola Road to Green Valley Trucktrail.

Dos Picos Regional Park
Dos Picos Park Road
✦ Take I-8 to SR76 north. Take SR76 to Mussey Grade Road south. Turn west onto Dos Picos Park Road and take it to the park.

Lake Poway Recreation Area
✦ Take I-15 to Espola Road (S5) east. Take Espola Road to Lake Poway Road east to Lake Poway.

SAN DIEGO

Balboa Park
Balboa Drive & El Prado
✦ Take I-5 to 163 north to Quince Street exit. Take Quince Street to Balboa Drive.

Chollas Lake Park
6350 College Grove Drive
✦ Take I-5 to 94 east to College Avenue north. Turn west on College Grove Drive to 6350 College Grove Drive.

Florida Canyon
Morley Field Drive and Jacaranda Drive
✧ Take I-5 to Pershing Drive. Take Pershing Drive and turn north onto Florida Street north. Take Florida Street to Morley Field Drive and turn right. Head up to Jacaranda Drive and park.

Kate O. Sessions Park
5115 Soledad Road at Park Drive
✧ Take I-5 to Garnet Avenue west. Take Garnet Avenue to Lamont Street north. Lamont Street turns into Soledad Road at Beryl Street. Continue north on Soledad Road to Park Drive.

Lake Miramar
Scripps Lake Drive
✧ Take I-15 to Mira Mesa Boulevard east. Take Mira Mesa Boulevard to Scripps Ranch Boulevard south. Take Scripps Ranch Boulevard to Scripps Lake Drive and park at the library.

Los Penasquitos Canyon Preserve
12020 Black Mountain Road
✧ Take I-15 to Mercy Road west. Take Mercy Road to Black Mountain Road.

Marian Bear Memorial Park
Regents Road off Route 52
✧ Take I-5 to Route 52 to the Regents Road exit. Entrance to the park to is south of Route 52.

Mission Trails Regional Park
8102 Father Junipero Serra Trail
✧ Take I-8 to Mission Gorge Road exit north. Head north till you see the entrance at Father Juniper Serra Trail.

Presidio Park
2811 Jackson Street
✧ Take I-8 to Taylor Street west. Take Taylor Street to Jackson Street.

If you have an older dog or puppy, don't overwork them while hiking. They tire easily and it won't be enjoyable to either one of you.

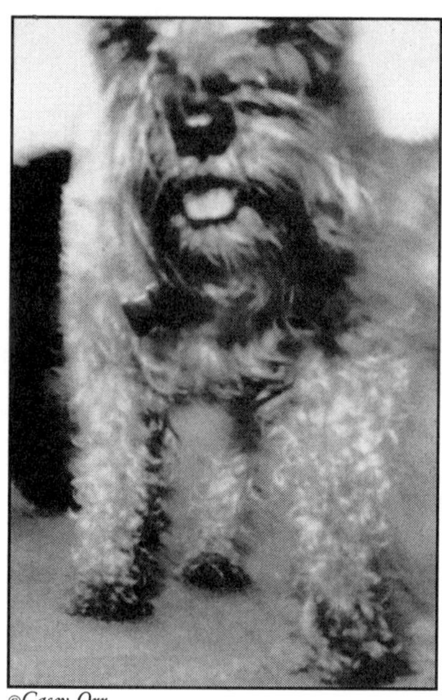

©Casey Orr

Invest in a retractable leash. This will give your dog more room to explore while not constantly interrupting your own exploration.

Rose Canyon
8000 block Genessee Avenue
✦ Take I-5 to 52 east. Take Genesee Avenue north. Open space will be on the left.

Tecolote Canyon Natural Park
Tecolote Road off Morena Boulevard
✦ Take I-8 to Morena Boulevard north. Take Morena Boulevard to Tecolote Road east.

SANTA YSIBEL

Inaja Memorial Park
✦ Take I-15 to 78 east. Take 78 east to 78/79 east. Park is at the 5000 block of Julian Road between Santa Ysabel and Wynola.

SOLANA BEACH

San Dieguito Park
1628 Lomas Santa Fe Drive
✦ Take I-5 to Lomas Santa Fe Drive (S8) exit. Head east and park at 1628 Lomas Santa Fe Drive near Sun Valley Road.

San Elijo Lagoon Wildlife Reserve
✦ Take I-5 to Lomas Santa Fe Drive east. Turn north onto Santa Helena. Turn north onto Santa Victoria. Turn north onto Santa Carina to the end.

©Casey Orr

SWEETWATER

Sweetwater County Park
3218 Summit Meadow Road
✦ Take 805 to Bonita Road (S17) east to San Miguel Road east. Turn north on Summit Meadow Road to the end.

VALLEY CENTER

Hellhole
Kiavo Road
✦ Take I-15 to Valley Center Road (S6) east. Take Lake Wolford Road south to Paradise Mountain Road east to Kiavo Road north.

NOTES

NOTES

Chapter Four

©Casey Orr

Grooming

Grooming

Exercise is an important part of keeping a healthy, happy pet. But, after all those hikes and trips to the beach, you are bound to end up with a dusty, smelly dog. Proper grooming is very important to ensure your pet's health and happiness. Your companion animal will not only look better, but will also be physically and psychologically healthier.

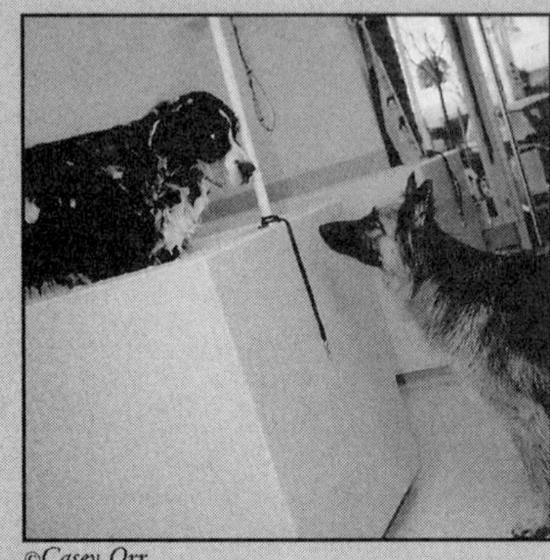

©Casey Orr

There are many choices in dog grooming these days. Depending on your dog's needs, you can choose between a full service salon, a self-service pet wash, or even a mobile grooming service.

A full service salon will offer shampooing, of course, but also brushing, ear cleaning, anal gland expressing, nail clipping, coat conditioning, even styling. Your dog will come out looking and smelling ready for a dog show. Certain breeds require professional grooming, but all dogs can benefit from a full-service grooming service.

If you are more the do-it-yourself type, you can choose a self-service pet wash. These places are good choices for those who have larger dogs, or those who desire a professionally cleaned animal but don't have the tools to do it themselves. You'll be provided with a place to bath your dog, brushes, and all the equipment you'll need for a nominal fee. Some have groomers on hand to handle the more difficult tasks such as nail clipping.

Some dogs are very nervous about grooming, and if that is the case, the best option might be to choose a mobile cleaning service. A professional groomer in a fully equipped van will come to your home and do the job right in your driveway. Being at home soothes a nervous pet and gives the owner the satisfaction of having a hygienic dog as well.

In this next chapter, we'll fully detail the grooming options available to you in San Diego.

ALPINE

Alpine Animal Jungle Grooming
1730 Alpine Boulevard
(619) 445-4000

CARLSBAD

Bark Shoppe
576 Carlsbad Village Drive
(760) 729-1708

Karen's Custom Grooming
7130 Avenida Encinas, Suite 100
(760) 431-7553

Lucky Pup The
2786 State Street
(760) 729-3198

Mohnacky Animal Hospital
2505 S. Vista Way
(760) 729-3330

Muddy Paws
2624 El Camino Real
(760) 434-0268

Pacific Coast K-9's Seacrest Kennels
7250 Ponto Drive
(760) 438-2469

CORONADO

Pollyanna Grooming Parlour
1108 10th Street
(619) 435-4934

DEL MAR

Curry Comb The
1210 Camino Del Mar
(858) 755-2677

©Casey Orr

Inspect your dog after grooming to make sure he or she wasn't harmed. If your dog seems scared or if there are nicks or cuts, your pet may have been abused. If the dog seems lethargic, he may have been given a sedative without your permission. Discuss these things with your groomer and ask for references. If other dogs have gone through the same thing, a report should be filed with the Humane Society and/or S.P.C.A.

©Casey Orr

You should always brush your dog thoroughly everyday. This keeps your dog's coat from getting tangled, removes dirt, spreads natural oils and keeps the skin clean. Be gentle and reward your dog afterwards by giving them praise and/or a treat.

PETCO
2749 Via De La Valle
(858) 259-0110
www.petco.com

EL CAJON

A Town & Country Mobile Groomer
1428 Broadway
(619) 401-9050

Angel's Pet Parlor
2471 Jamacha Road
(619) 444-9490

Barbara's Grooming
1137 N. 2nd Street
(619) 579-1830

Beth's Pet Spa
1028 Broadway
(619) 588-2726

Bonnie's Grooming
1215 N. 2nd Street
(619) 588-6123

Broadway Animal Hospital
380 Broadway
(619) 444-1166

Classy Canine School of Dog Grooming
723 E. Bradley Avenue
(619) 449-4443

Cricket Ridge Kennels
1329 E. Chase Avenue
(619) 447-8020

PETCO
540 N. 2nd Street
(619) 441-5200
www.petco.com

PETCO
2510 Jamacha Boulevard
(619) 670-9688 • www.petco.com

Petsmart
865 Jackman Street
(619) 442-6661
www.petsmart.com

Rancho San Diego Animal Hospital
2988 Jamacha Road
(619) 660-6767

Shear Perfection by Wendy
1325 E. Main Street
(619) 447-7366

Tender Loving Care Pet Salon
1428 Broadway
(619) 447-6585

ENCINITAS

Alcala Pet Care
1273 Crest Drive
(760) 436-6619
www.alcalapetcare.com

Animal Keeper The
155 Saxony Road
(760) 753-9366
www.animalkeeper.com

Carm's Pet Grooming
2141 Newcastle Avenue
(760) 436-4573

Dogs in Suds
382 N. El Camimo Real
(760) 943-0653

Holiday Pet Hotel & The Cat's Pajamas
551 Union Street
(760) 753-6754

PETCO
154 Encinitas Boulevard
(760) 632-6600
www.petco.com

You should bathe your dog every other month. However, your dog may need additional bathing if he is active, plays in the dirt or is constantly smelly. Keep in mind though, body odor may be a symptom of another problem. Check with your groomer or veterinarian if the problem persists.

©Casey Orr

Check with your veterinarian if these symptoms occur to your dogs ears:

- *Constant scratching of the ears.*
- *Constant shaking of the head.*
- *Red, black or brown inside the ear.*
- *Foul odor.*

Dirty ears can become infected, causing pain or hearing loss.

Petsmart
1034 N. El Camino Real
(760) 436-2048
www.petsmart.com

Puppy Love Pet Spa
191 N. El Camino Real
(760) 634-1559

ESCONDIDO

4 Feet & Feathers
1835 S. Centre City Parkway
(760) 480-0858

A Master's Touch Pet Wash
555 Country Club Lane
(760) 740-9274
www.amasterstouch.com

Animal Medical Hospital of Escondido
130 N. Hale Avenue
(760) 741-8221

Cathy's Canine
2205 E. Valley Parkway, #D
(760) 745-1700

Cold Nose Grooming Salon & Boutique
254 W. 8th Avenue
(760) 741-2707

PETCO
1050 W. Valley Parkway
(760) 781-1600
www.petco.com

Raining Cats and Dogs
1911 Sunset Drive
(760) 743-0136

Shampoodle
1330 E. Valley Parkway
(760) 489-1559

FALLBROOK

Country Grooming
112 W. Beech Street
(760) 723-2707

Fallbrook Animal Lodge
1115 E. Mission Road
(760) 728-0892

Lovin' Friends Grooming
1227 S. Mission Road
(760) 728-8647

Pampered Pets
1672 S. Mission Road
(760) 723-2332

IMPERIAL BEACH

Margaret's Pet Wash
600 Palm Avenue, Suite 114
(619) 429-3797

LA COSTA

Aloha Mobile Pet Salon
(760) 804-0787

LA MESA

Andy's Pet Salon
7732 University Avenue
(619) 698-4933

Aunt Lisa's Grooming Parlor
7520 El Cajon Boulevard
(619) 466-9580

Bark Avenue Pet Salon
3657 Avocado Boulevard
(619) 670-9422

Barking Lot, The
7991 La Mesa Boulevard
(619) 697-2284

©Casey Orr

To clean your own dog's ears, take a cotton swab or soft cloth, moisten it with warm water and put a little mineral oil on it. Make your dog feel comfortable and safe, lift the ear flaps and clean the canal and flaps with the cotton ball or cloth. Make sure not to go too deep into the canals.

Make your dog feel comfortable while brushing your dog by letting him smell the brush, talking to him in a calm tone, and petting his comfortable spot. Then start brushing from head to toe in the direction of the hair growth. Various brushes and combs can be used to take care of your particular dog's coat and various problems such as tangles and mats. Ask your groomer which product is best for your dog.

La Mesa Pet Hotel
8126 Center Street
(619) 466-6166
www.lamesa-pethotel.com

Lake Murray Grooming
6020 Lake Murray Boulevard
(619) 462-7297

Nikki's Neat & Trim Pet Grooming
8681 La Mesa Boulevard
(619) 589-1106

Pampered Paws Grooming Salon
8127 La Mesa Boulevard
(619) 466-1274

Tami's Tender Touch
8818 La Mesa Boulevard
(619) 465-7387

LAKESIDE

Carter Kennels
8755 Winter Gardens Boulevard
(619) 561-1464

Paw's Place Grooming
13334 Highway 8 Business
(619) 443-3647

Varsity Kennels
8447 Winter Gardens Boulevard
(619) 561-3037

LAKESIDE FARMS

Marlene's Grooming Shop
12227 Woodside Avenue
(619) 390-6482

LEMON GROVE

Grooming by Trish
7572 North Avenue
(619) 464-0997

M & M's Family Pet Grooming
7249 Broadway
(619) 466-5215

NATIONAL CITY

Fiesta Pet Shop
1145 Highland Avenue
(619) 477-5997

Pet Plaza
911 E. Plaza Boulevard
(619) 477-4076

Plaza Boulevard Pet Hospital & Grooming
2415 E. Plaza Boulevard
(619) 267-8200
www.petcaretotheheart.com

OCEANSIDE

1st Klass Pet Salon
1820 Marron Road
(760) 434-7560

Animal Keeper The
3532 College Boulevard
(760) 941-3221
www.animalkeeper.com

Classy Clips
3375 Mission Avenue, #G
(760) 721-1562

Dippity-Dog Pet Wash & Self Serve Pet Wash
2216 El Camino Real
(760) 439-3313
www.dippity-dog.com

Groomingdale's
2805 Oceanside Boulevard
(760) 757-6477

Mohnacky Animal Hospital
3504-E College Boulevard
(760) 945-1000

©Casey Orr

Some dogs are allergic to fleas, like Jane. If your dog has a bad allergic reaction to flea bites or any other type bites and he becomes rash ridden, use some Bag Balm on the rash. It's an ointment used for cow utters. It's nonpoisonous and soothes the irritation, making your dog less likely to scratch. You don't want your dog to be uncomfortable and get into the repetitive habit of scratching. Scratching can lead to sores and ripped skin which is all together another problem for you and your dog.

Debbie, Owner
Pet Paradise

©Casey Orr

Regularly scheduled grooming appointments on a monthly basis may reduce the cost of your grooming bill. Ask you groomer if he or she can offer you any discounts or plans.

Oceana Pet Stop
563 Vista Bella
(760) 439-6060

PETCO
2445 Vista Way
(760) 967-7387
www.petco.com

PETCO
3875 Mission Avenue
(760) 754-1400
www.petco.com

Tails A Waggin'
612 S. Coast Highway
(760) 722-0811

The Dog Father
425 South Nevada Street
(760) 757-6858

POWAY

Agape Professional Grooming & Pet Sitting
1344 Community Road
(858) 513-8373

Animal Keeper The
12280 Oak Knoll Road
(858) 748-9676
www.animalkeeper.com

Beauty and the Beast Pet Grooming
14025 Poway Road
(858) 679-9559

Dapper Doggery
12855 Pomerado Road
(858) 748-7554

Lucky Dog Pet Wash & Pet Sitting
13248 Poway Road
(858) 486-8056

Lucky Dog Professional Grooming
13248 Poway Road
(858) 486-9832

PETCO
13375 Poway Road
(858) 679-2020
www.petco.com

RAMONA

A Country Clip Pet Grooming
2021 Main Street
(760) 788-3722

Animal Artistry's Grooming & Boarding
202 6th Avenue
(760) 789-7436

For Pet Sake Dog Grooming
19990 Indian Oaks Road
(760) 789-4023

Kathy's Country Pet Shop
1520 Main Street
(760) 789-6272

Rainbow Grooming Plus
332 'B' Street
(760) 789-7722

RANCHO BERNARDO

West Bernardo Grooming
11605 Duenda Road
(858) 451-1815

RANCHO SANTA FE

Animal First Pet Beauty Parlor
Helen Woodward Animal Center
6461 El Apajo Road
(858) 756-5545

SAN DIEGO

A Cut Above Pet Grooming
2933 Lincoln Avenue
(619) 692-0721

"Educate yourself about your dog, and your dog will educate you about yourself."

Donna F. Walker, Owner
South Bark Dog Wash
Southpark, San Diego

©Casey Orr

©Casey Orr

If you have a longer haired dog, you should probably take it to the groomer every 6-12 weeks for professional grooming. This maintenance grooming schedule should include you brushing your dog thoroughly everyday.

A Pet's Best Friend
3251 Greyling Drive
(858) 278-1909

AAA Pet Professionals
508 Nautilus, La Jolla
(858) 456-1552

All About Animals
5622 La Jolla Boulevard, La Jolla
(858) 459-4583

All About Grooming
7525 Mission Gorge Road
(619) 583-3644

All Breed Dog & Cat Grooming
11295 Camino Ruiz
(858) 271-1542

Animal Attraction
3386 Governor Drive
(858) 587-1677

Animal Center of San Diego
246 West Washington
(619) 299-7387

Best Friends Pet Resort & Salon
8020 Ronson Road
(858) 565-8055

Best Of Breed Grooming
4503 Alabama
(619) 299-9244

Best Yet Dog Grooming
3117 54th
(619) 287-9678

Better Grooming
4804 Gallatin Way
(858) 272-4301

Camp Diego
2926 Garnet Avenue, Pacific Beach
(619) 224-2267

Canine Cleaners
10448 Clairemont Mesa Boulevard, Pacific Beach
(858) 503-6727

Canine Coiffures
5155 La Jolla Boulevard, Pacific Beach
(858) 459-2888

Canine Image
3520 Ashford Street
(858) 279-3336

Casa de Pets
3915 Ohio Street
(619) 297-4646

Center Veterinary Clinic
8977 Mira Mesa Boulevard
(858) 271-1152

Christine's Pet Grooming
4239 Park Boulevard
(619) 299-6410

Classic Grooming of La Jolla
7760 Fay Avenue, La Jolla
(858) 459-0302

Clippindale's Grooming Gallery
5401 Linda Vista Road, Suite 409
(619) 291-2855

Critter Cleaners
9870 Hibert Street
(858) 566-7890

Dapper Dog by Tiara
5514 La Jolla Boulevard
(858) 488-9500

Debonair Dog
3949 Clairemont Drive
(858) 272-4083

If your dog is covered with burrs after a day of hiking, give her a bath with lots of conditioner. Brush or comb your pooch with the conditioner in her coat. This makes it easier to pick or brush the burrs out.

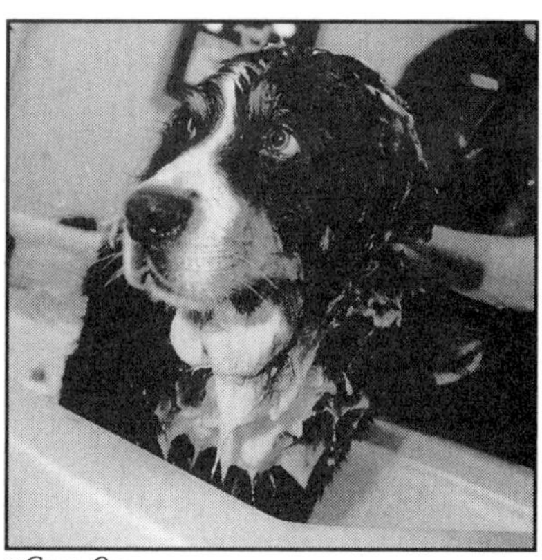

©Casey Orr

If you or your child contracts head lice, don't be afraid that your dog will get it too and vice versa. Human lice can only live on humans so take care of your house (cleaning carpets, furniture, sheets, clothing, stuffed animals, etc.) as if you would if you didn't have a dog. Don't treat your dog with anything except "for-dog" treatments, if necessary. The same goes for dog lice . . . it can not live on humans.

©Casey Orr

Doggie Station
8951 Carlton Hills Boulevard
(619) 449-2346

Dirty Paws
6030 Santo Road, Tierra Santa
(858) 569-7387

Dog Beach Dog Wash
4933 Voltaire Street
(619) 523-1700
www.dogwash.com

Dog Care Grooming Center
5622 La Jolla Boulevard, La Jolla
(858) 459-4583

Dog Gone Gorgeous
(619) 302-3647

Doggie Detailers Mobile Grooming
(619) 235-0050

Exotic Pooch The
969 Hornblend Street
(858) 274-8660

Fon Jon Kennels
5050 Santa Fe Street
(858) 273-2266

Golden Paw The
5305 Metro Street
(619) 299-2730
www.TheGoldenPaw.net

Grooming Cottage
4670 Park Boulevard
(619) 260-1892

Groomingdales of Kensington
4110 Adams Avenue
(619) 584-6472

Hair of the Dog
4783 Narragansett Avenue
(619) 223-3080

Joyce's Dog Grooming
4611 Seda Drive
(858) 560-7646

Maggie's Farm Natural Pet Grooming
3786 Rosecrans
(619) 220-8683

Mission Valley Kennels
4325 Twain Avenue
(619) 282-0022

My Beautiful Dog-O-Mat
3789 Park Boulevard
(619) 295-6140

Noah's Ark Pet Wash
4431 Cass Street - Pacific Beach
(619) 270-8161

Ocean Beach Dog Wash
4933 Voltaire
(619) 523-1700

Pacific Beach Pet Salon
1964 Garnet Avenue, Pacific Beach
(858) 274-8844

Paw Alley
2535 Clairemont Drive
(619) 276-3093

Paw Spa for Dogs & Cats The
6690 Mission Gorge Road
(619) 284-7387

Penasquitos Pets
13223 Black Mountain Road
(858) 484-3809

Pet Palace The
3827 Ray Street, North Park
(619) 291-6565

Pet Paradise
2923 Upas Street, North Park
(619) 299-1810

©Casey Orr

Should you tip your groomer? Well, if the groomer is also the store owner, the general rule of thumb is no. But if they did an excellent job, you may want to give a little extra. If the groomer isn't, then 10-20% of the bill would be appropriate, depending on how frequent you go and how difficult of a job they had.

©Casey Orr

If you groom your own dogs using blades, get the blades sharpened professionally. In the long run, you avoid the risk of ruining your own blades and you can have the piece of mind that they will be sharpened correctly. Ask your local groomer who they use to sharpen their blades.

Pet Pawlor of Rancho Bernardo
12540 Oaks North Drive
(858) 673-1777

PETCO
3994 Clairemont Mesa Boulevard
(858) 483-4100
www.petco.com

PETCO
7375 Jackson Drive
(619) 697-8200
www.petco.com

PETCO
11160 Rancho Carmel Drive
(858) 451-8347
www.petco.com

PETCO
8610 Genesee Avenue
(858) 550-0973
www.petco.com

PETCO
8160 Mira Mesa Boulevard
(858) 635-5800
www.petco.com

PETCO
1210 West Morena Boulevard
(619) 275-5100
www.petco.com

PETCO
10410 Friars Road
(619) 563-0071
www.petco.com

Petland Grooming
5430 Clairemont Mesa Boulevard
(858) 268-3721

Petmarket
6363 El Cajon Boulevard
(619) 286-3474

Pets Best Friend
3251 Greyling Drive
(858) 278-1909

Petsmart
3396 Murphy Canyon Road
(858) 571-0083

Petsmart
3610 Rosecrans Street
(619) 523-4180
www.petsmart.com

Pink Poodle Pet Salon
6134 El Cajon Boulevard
(619) 583-2261

Poochies Dog Wash and Espresso Bar
6030 Santo Road
(858) 541-2663

Preferred by Pets
3903 Voltaire Street
(619) 223-9023

Prestige Dog Grooming
1108 Calle de Vida
(858) 560-7646

Priscilla's Grooming
8181 Mission Gorge Road
(619) 265-7422

Robin's Dog House
3904 Convoy Street
(858) 279-2251

Sandy's Animal Services
(858) 273-6022

Satin Scissors of Point Loma & Ocean
3904 Convey
(619) 224-2223

Shear Delite
818 Fort Stockton Drive
(619) 297-3470

Don't overbathe your dog. It will dry out their skin and coat, making them feel itchy and irritable. This will lead to excessive scratching which could become a bad habit.

©Casey Orr

Your dog's nails should be trimmed about once a month. Buy a nail clipper specifically for your type of dog, blood-clotting powder and cotton balls, and follow these steps:

- *Take your dog's paw into your hands.*
- *Cut one nail at a time. Do not cut into the quick, the part of the nail that has the nerves and blood vessels.*
- *If you do cut into the quick, use the clotting powder on a cotton ball and apply it on the cut.*
- *After you have trimmed all the claws, trim the dewclaws. They are located inside of the front legs.*

Snooty's Classic Grooming
1110 Torrey Pines Road, La Jolla
(858) 454-8020

South Bark Dog Wash
2037 30th Street
(619) 232-7387
www.southbark.com

Susie's Pet Clipet
4433 Park Boulevard
(619) 260-1030

Teddy's Dog House
5589 Clairemont Mesa Boulevard
(858) 292-8676

You Dirty Dog - Mission Hills Salon
(619) 297-6299

Yuko's Dog Grooming
3928 Iowa Street
(619) 280-6040

SAN MARCOS

California School of Dog Grooming
655 S. Rancho Santa Fe
(760) 949-3746

Grooming by Beth
740 Nordahl Road
(760) 432-0877

Mohnacky Animal Hospital
997 W. San Marcos Boulevard, 102A
(760) 744-0032

Paw-Dre's Clubhouse for Pets
1049 E. Mission Road
(760) 745-2759
www.sdco-op.com/pets

PETCO
1609 Capalina Road
(760) 752-1300
www.petco.com

Petite Pet Parlour
1241 W. San Marcos Boulevard
(760) 744-1335

A Supergroom
7601 Draper Avenue, La Jolla
(858) 483-4680

Village Groomers
1145 San Marino Drive, #143
(760) 744-2545

Ye Olde Poodle Parlour
740 Nordahl Road
(760) 745-9471

SANTEE

Bostone's Doggy Shop
8781 Cuyamaca Street
(619) 449-6400

Carlton Hills Grooming
8951 Carlton Hills Boulevard
(619) 562-7760

Lakeside Dog Grooming
11555 Woodside Avenue
(619) 562-0710

PETCO
9851 Buena Vista Avenue
(619) 596-5900
www.petco.com

S U - E T S Kennels -Scottish Terriers
10631 Prospect Avenue
(619) 448-8760

Westwinds Grooming
10251 Mast Boulevard
(619) 448-8642

SOLANA BEACH

Charlie's Canine Corner
574 Stevens Avenue
(858) 755-5222

Teeth cleaning should be an important part of your dog's grooming regimen. Clean your dog's teeth at least twice a week using a doggie toothpaste on a soft-bristled toothbrush. This will combat cavities and other periodontal diseases.

©Casey Orr

©Casey Orr

When bathing your dog, do not spray water into his or her face or forcefully at the anal glands.

Perfect Pet Salon
201 S. Highway 101
(858) 755-3308

Pet Spa
247 S. Highway 101
(858) 755-9318

Professional Grooming Do It Yourself Dog
112 West Plaza
(858) 755-7778

Rancho-Solana Pet Spa
247 S. Highway 101
(858) 755-9318

Solana Beach Do It Yourself Dog Wash
112 W. Plaza
(858) 755-7778

SPRING VALLEY

Bark Park
3971 Spring Drive
(619) 461-5577

Mike's Aquarium & Pet Centers
651 Sweetwater Road
(619) 461-7661

Plaza Pet
9734-1/2 Campo Road
(619) 466-6320

Spring Creek Kennel and Cattery
9279 Campo Road
(619) 463-1722

VALLEY CENTER

Alibi Acres Kennels
16750 Paradise Mountain Road
(760) 749-4100

Countryside Veterinary Clinic
28746 Valley Center Road
(760) 749-3656

Pup's N Bubbles
29030 Lilac Road
(760) 749-0161

VISTA

Brengle Terrace Animal Hospital
971 Vale Terrace Drive
(760) 758-8004

Canine Castle Dog Boarding
814 Crest View Road
(760) 726-2068
www.caninecastle.com

Ce Ce Belle Pet Hotel
29920 Margale Lane
(760) 758-7322

Country Feed Grooming Room
2111 E. Vista Way
(760) 724-6421

Mickey's K-9 Country Club
1920 Shadowridge Drive
(760) 727-1278

PETCO
520 Hacienda Drive
(760) 631-5770 • www.petco.com

Petsmart
1740 University Drive
(760) 630-3361
www.petsmart.com

Spicer's Shaggy Dog
1929 W. Vista Way
(760) 726-7387

Tails A Waggin'
1318 N. Santa Fe Avenue
(760) 941-1991

Wag-N-Wheels
290 Puffin Drive
(760) 631-1696

Put cotton balls into your dog's ears when bathing your dog. This will prevent water getting into your dog's ear canals.

NOTES

Chapter Five

Shopping

Shopping

©Casey Orr

The joys of sharing your life with a canine companion are immeasurable, but there is a slight downside - it can be expensive. Being a responsible dog owner means purchasing supplies to keep your pet healthy and happy. Dog food will be on your list, but toys are important for training and fun. Bones and chews are necessary for healthy teeth, and you may at times need new leashes, bowls and grooming supplies as well as other accessories.

You can inject some fun into these purchases by bringing your dog along. Many pet stores will allow you and your pooch to browse together. Puppies in particular love the variety of scents and textures contained within these stores. Taking your dog shopping is not only a great way to get the supplies you need, but also an excellent way to socialize your pet.

There are many places within San Diego that you and your pet can go to shop together. The major superstores will have all the accessories you need conveniently arranged by type of animal. Some also have onsite grooming, veterinary services, and pet adoptions. There are also dozens of smaller stores within the county that cater just to dog lovers. These stores specialize in everything from homemade dog bones to handmade doggie sweaters.

In the coming pages, we'll list these stores for you, from the well known to the hidden gem. You'll find out where to find that jeweled collar and where to get that peanut butter flavored bone your pooch craves.

Taking a well-behaved dog to a friendly store is an entertaining experience for both of you. You may end up enjoying it so much you won't notice the cost!

ALPINE

Alpine Animal Jungle
1730 Alpine Boulevard
(619) 445-4022

CARLSBAD

Richlin Farms Pet Nutrition
6949 El Camino Real
(760) 804-7387

Wesco - Carlsbad Pet Supplies
2855 Roosevelt
(760) 434-0930

CHULA VISTA

PETCO
11 4th Avenue
(619) 427-2112
www.petco.com

CORONADO

PETCO
925 Orange Avenue
(619) 437-6557
www.petco.com

Wag'n Tails
945 Orange Avenue
(619) 435-3513
www.wtpets.com

DEL MAR

Daily Pet, Inc.
12845 El Camino Real
(858) 481-2065

Dexter's Deli
1229 Camino Del Mar
(858) 792-3707
www.dextersdeli.com

"After acquiring a new dog or puppy, don't feel as though you need to buy everything in sight. Instead, start out with one comfort toy to find out what your new companion likes. Not all dogs like all types of toys."

Heather, Owner
Wag'n Tails
Coronado

"One thing I learned from my kids is that to keep your dog food fresh and pest free, especially from ants, is to invest in a "Vittle Vault" or something similar, sold at your local pet store. The vault doesn't burp but it seals with a reassuring sssssshhhhhh sound"

Lynda Pfeifer
Dutch, Imported German Shepherd from Germany
North Park

©Casey Orr

Mary's Tack & Feed
3675 Via De La Valle
(858) 755-2015
www.marystack.com

PETCO
2749 Via De La Valle
(858) 259-0110
www.petco.com

EL CAJON

Pet Nutrition Center
1265 Avocado, Suite 103
(619) 593-7387

PETCO
2510 Jamacha Road
(619) 670-9688
www.petco.com

PETCO
540 North 2nd Street
(619) 441-5200
www.petco.com

Petsmart
865 Jackman
(619) 442-6661
www.petsmart.com

ENCINITAS

Environgentle
543 Southcoast HWY 101
(760) 753-7420
www.environgentle.com

Invisible Fence of San Diego
1462 Encinitas Boulevard
(760) 633-4050

PETCO
154 Encinitas Boulevard
(760) 632-6600
www.petco.com

Petsmart
1034 N. El Camino Real
(760) 436-1220
www.petsmart.com

Richlin Pet Nutrition Center
123 North El Camino Real, Suite J
(760) 436-1226

ESCONDIDO

4 Feet & Feathers Pet Store
1835 S. Centre City Parkway #G
(760) 480-0858
www.4feetandfeatherspetshop.com

A Master's Touch Pet Wash
555 W. Country Club Lane
(760) 740-9274
www.uwashpet.com

Hawthorne Country Store
675 W. Grand Avenue
(760) 746-7816
www.hawthornecountrystore.com

PETCO
1000 West Valley Parkway
(760) 781-1600
www.petco.com

Shampoodle
1330 E. Valley Parkway
(760) 489-1559

FALLBROOK

Creature Comforts
131 W. Beech
(760) 723-1411

DJ Feed & Pet Supplies
232 W. Aviation Road
(760) 731-6080

©Casey Orr

Never leave your dog in a hot car. This can quickly cause heat stroke.

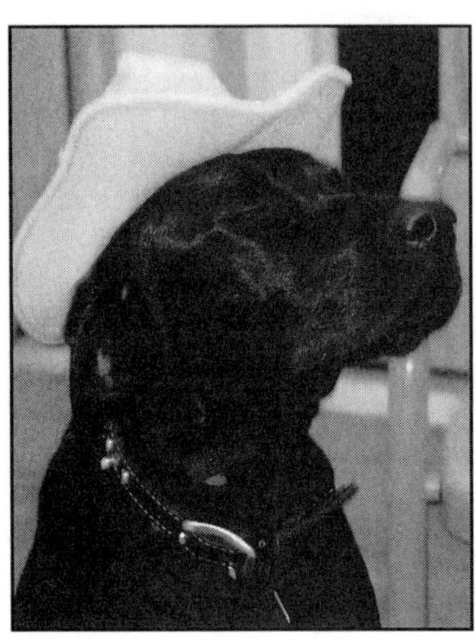

If your dog has an accident on the store floor, offer to clean it up.

L & M Feed
1043 E. Mission Road
(760) 723-3333

LA MESA

Pet Works
5500 Grossmont Center Drive
(619) 465-4446
www.pet/works.com

PETCO
8501 Fletcher Parkway
www.petco.com

PetPeople
8011 University Avenue
(619) 464-3757
www.petpeople.com

LEMON GROVE

Dave's Feed Shop
3655 Costabella
(619) 462-3434

NATIONAL CITY

Fiesta Pet Shop
1145 Highland Avenue
(619) 477-5997

Pet Plaza
911 E. Boulevard
(619) 477-4076

OCEANSIDE

Dog Father, The
425 South Nevada Street
(760) 757-6858

FTI Pet Products
P.O. Box 969
(760) 433-3888
www.fleatreat.com

Pet Supply Warehouse
3875 Mission Avenue
(760) 754-1211

PETCO
3875 Mission Avenue
(760) 754-1400
www.petco.com

PETCO
2445 West Vista Way
(760) 967-7387
www.petco.com

PetPeople
4170 Oceanside Boulevard
(760) 630-6130
www.petpeople.com

POWAY

PETCO
13375 Poway Road
(858) 679-2020

RAMONA

Animal Pharm
1668 Main Street
(760) 788-0286

Diamond D Feed & Supply
444 'D' Street
(760) 789-1240

Kathy's Country Pet Shop
1520 Main St.
(760) 789-6272
www.ramona.com under business

Paul's Pet Food Delivery Express
P.O. Box 1381
(760) 787-9991
www.paulspetfood.com

If you lead a holistic life, many stores offer all natural products for pets as well. Check out some of the specialty stores for these products and premium dog foods.

Before going out and buying an expensive doggie first-aid kit, make one your own. Visit a store that sells these kits, note what's in these kits and buy the individual items at your local pharmacy.

SAN DIEGO

A Pets Best Friend
3251 Greyling
(858) 278-1909

Ace - Hillcrest Hardware Inc.
1007 University Avenue
(619) 291-5988

America's Finest Pet Doors
(800) 826-2871

Animal House Pet Store
2726 University Avenue
(619) 295-8834

Cabrillo Pet Care Center
4130 Voltaire Street
(619) 224-9516

Dapper Dog by Tiara
5514 La Jolla Boulevard
(858) 488-9500
www.dapperdog.com

Dog Beach Dog Wash
4933 Voltaire Street
(619) 523-1700
www.dogwash.com

Golden Paw, The
5305 Metro Street
(619) 299-2730
www.goldenpaw.net

K9 & Co.
832 24th Street
(619) 544-1009

La Jolla Paws Pet Supply
7514 Girard Avenue
(858) 459-6614

Lil Raskals Family Pet Center
8440 Rio San Diego Drive
(619) 298-3057

Lil Raskals Family Pet Center
7514 Girard Avenue, Suite 3
(858) 459-6614

Maggie's Farm Natural Pet
3786 Rosecrans Street
(619) 220-8683

MX Dog Treats
8515 Arjons Drive
(858) 547-4180

My Beautiful Dog-O-Mat
3789 Park Boulevard
(619) 295-6140

Newport Pet
4896 Newport Avenue
(619) 224-6151

Original Paw Pleasers, The
1220 Cleveland Avenue, Suite M117
(619) 293-7297
www.pawpleasers.com

Penasquitos Pets
13223 Black Mountain Road
(858) 484-3809

Pet Express
(800) 735-7387

Pet Kingdom
3191 Sports Arena Boulevard
(619) 224-2841

Pet Stop
7490 La Jolla Boulevard
(858) 456-6311

PETCO
11160 Rancho Carmel Drive
(858) 451-8347
www.petco.com

Many stores have frequent buyers programs that can save you money. Ask your stores about available programs.

If there's a store not listed here, it does not mean they aren't dog-friendly. Call your favorite store and ask the management if it's okay to bring your dog.

PETCO
1945 Garnet Avenue
(858) 483-5821
www.petco.com

PETCO
8610 Genesee Avenue
(858) 550-0686
www.petco.com

PETCO
10410 Friars Road
(619) 563-0071
www.petco.com

PETCO
1210 West Morena Boulevard
(619) 275-5100
www.petco.com

PETCO
3994 Clairemont Mesa Boulevard
(858) 483-4100
www.petco.com

PETCO
8160 Mira Mesa Boulevard
(858) 635-5800
www.petco.com

PETCO
7375 Jackson Drive
(619) 687-8200
www.petco.com

Petland Grooming
5430 Clairemont Mesa Boulevard
(858) 268-3721

Petmarket
6363 El Cajon Boulevard
(619) 286-3474

Petmarket
635 Saturn Boulevard
(619) 575-7387

Pet Me, Please
3401 Adams Avenue
(619) 283-5020

PetPeople
5664 Mission Center Road
(619) 291-7223
www.petpeople.com

PetPeople
1786 Garnet Avenue
(858) 270-3499
www.petpeople.com

PetPeople
3625 Midway Drive
(619) 523-0552
www.petpeople.com

PetPeople
8843 Villa La Jolla Drive
(858) 457-2036
www.petpeople.com

Petsmart
3396 Murphy Canyon Road
(858) 571-0083
www.petsmart.com

Petsmart
3610 Rosecrans Street
(619) 523-4180
www.petsmart.com

Pink Poodle Pet Salon
6134 El Cajon Boulevard
(619) 583-8861

Richlin Farms Pet Nutrition
3840 Valley Centre Drive
(858) 259-1777

Robin's Dog House
3904 Convoy Street
(858) 279-2251

If you know a store is going to be busy at a particular time, you may not want to take your dog with you or wait till to go when the store's less busy.

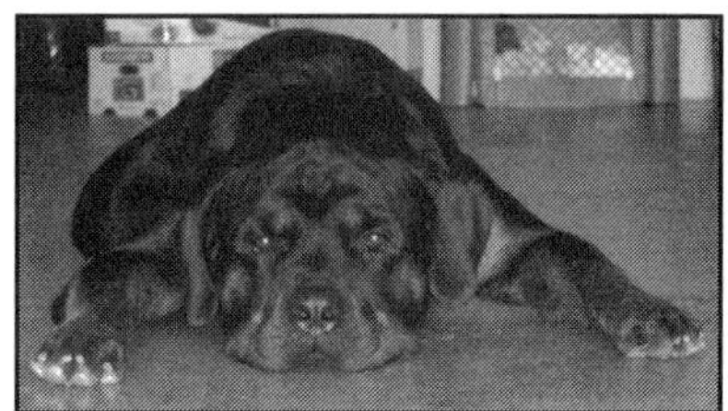

San Diego Pet Supply
4580 Federal Boulevard
(619) 263-2211

South Bark Dog Wash, LLC
2037 30th Street
(619) 232-7387
www.southbark.com

SAN MARCOS

Ye Olde Poodle Parlour
740 Nordahl Road
(760) 745-9471

SANTEE

All 4 Pets
9710 Mission Gorge Road
(619) 258-1030

East County Feed & Supply
10845 Woodside Avenue
(619) 562-2208

PETCO
9851 Buena Vista Avenue
(619) 596-5900
www.petco.com

Don't allow your dog to rip open packaged goods or play with dog toys, unless you are willing to buy them.

SOLANA BEACH

Perfect Pet Salon
201 S. Highway 101
(858) 755-3308

Richlin Farms Pet Nutrition
134 S. Solana Hills Drive
(858) 259-0177

SPRING VALLEY

Mike's Aquarium & Pet Centers
651 Sweetwater Road
(619) 461-7661

Plaza Pet
9734-1/2 Campo Road
(619) 466-6320

VALLEY CENTER

4 My Dogs
(760) 731-9570

G & L Farm Supply
28520 Cole Grade Road
(760) 749-0113

VISTA

Country Feed Store
2111 E. Vista Way
(760) 724-6421

PETCO
520 Hacienda Drive
(760) 631-5770
www.petco.com

Petsmart
1740 University Drive
(760) 630-3544
www.petsmart.com

Many stores offer free sample treats. Take advantage of this by bringing your dog on an empty stomach. That way, you will know what types of treats your dog will like.

NOTES

Chapter Six

Restaurants & Coffee Houses

Restaurants and Coffee Houses

©Casey Orr

One of life's great pleasures is a steaming cup of coffee or a plate of eggs on a pleasant morning, spent in the company of a newspaper and your best friend. San Diego offers many restaurants and cafés that encourage you to break bread with your dog and enjoy this peaceful experience.

Of course, in keeping with the California style of cuisine, many dog-friendly restaurants dish up more then simple eggs and coffee. Gourmet goodies for you are served alongside delicacies for your doggie. Even restaurants that don't typically cater to the dog-loving crowd will often let you bring your pet, and sometimes even bring a bowl of water or a bone for your dog to enjoy.

Due to health laws, you and your dog will be dining al fresco, yet with San Diego's lovely weather, this presents no problem. Some dog-friendly restaurants offer an ocean view, others have patio gardens, and some have out front dining where you and pooch can watch the world walk by.

In this chapter we'll give you a listing of restaurants that welcome dogs. We do suggest that you call prior to heading out, as management and policies may quickly change.

CARDIFF BY THE SEA

Las Olas Mexican Restaurant
2655 S. Highway 101
(760) 942-1860
Dogs may be tied up to the straw umbrella outside the patio.

Miracles Cafe
1953 Elijo Road
(760) 943-7924
Dogs may be tied outside the patio.

CARLSBAD

It's Coffee Time
7160 Avenida Encinitas, Suite 100
(760) 942-1860
Dogs may be tied up to the straw umbrella outside the patio.

Jay's Gourmet Restaurant by the Sea
2366 S. Highway 101
(760) 634-3353

Spirito's Restaurant
300 Carlsbad Village Drive # 208
(760) 720-1132

CORONADO

Bay Beach Cafe
1201 1st Street #115
(619) 435-4900
Dogs are not allowed in the cafe, however there are shaded areas to tie your dog.

Cafe 1134
1134 Orange Avenue
(619) 437-1134

Coronado Bakery
1206 Orange Avenue
(619) 435-9272

©Casey Orr

"When taking your dog to a restaurant or coffee shop, keep him or her on the leash and close to you. This way, diners and waiters won't trip over or hurt your dog or themselves."

Tracy Ratliff, bartender
Dixie - Pitbull
Normal Heights

If someone approaches your dog and is not savvy about dogs, teach the other person about dogs and tell them to do the following things:

- *Approach a dog slowly.*
- *Do not lean over the dog.*
- *Speak in a calm voice.*
- *Get down to the dog's level.*
- *Let the dog come to you.*
- *Let the dog sniff your hand.*
- *Scratch the dog under its chin if the dog accepts you.*

Deli By The Bay
1201 1st Street #K5
(619) 437-1006

Primavera Pastry Cafe
956 Orange Avenue
(619) 435-4191

Rhinoceros Cafe and Grill
1166 Orange Avenue
(619) 435-2121

DEL MAR

A Garden Taste
1237 Camino Del Mar
(858) 793-1500

Il Forno
1555 Camino Del Mar
(858) 755-8876

Sbicca's - An American Bistro
215 15th Street
(858) 481-1001

Sammy's California Woodfired Pizza
12925 El Camino Real
(858) 259-6600

ENCINITAS

Potato Shack
120 West 'I' Street
(760) 436-1282

Sakura Bana Sushi Bar
1031 S. Coast Highway 101
(760) 942-6414

Swami's
1163 S. Coast Highway 101
(760) 944-0612

ESCONDIDO

Gaby's Bakery & Deli
113 E. Grand Road
(760) 480-6801

LA MESA

Caruso's Bar Roma
8201 La Mesa Boulevard
(619) 460-4800

Por Favor Mexican Restaurant
8302 La Mesa Boulevard
(619) 698-5950
Dogs may be tied up outside the patio.

LAKESIDE

The Golden Goose
10001 Maine Road
(619) 390-1990
Dogs may be tied up outside to the benches.

OCEANSIDE

Armenian Cafe
3126 Carlsbad Boulevard
(760) 720-2233

Beach Break Cafe
1902 S. Coast Highway
(760) 439-6355

Harbor Fish and Chips
276 Harbor Drive S.
(760) 722-4977

Hill Street Coffee House
524 Hill Street
(760) 966-0985

Johnny Mananas
308 Mission Avenue
(760) 721-9999

POWAY

Chicken Pie Diner
14727 Pomerado Road
(858) 748-2445

Papachino's
13425 Poway Road
(858) 748-7100

If your dog is the rowdy, impatient, or playful type that doesn't like to sit still for a period of time or isn't friendly, you should not bring your dog to a restaurant or coffee shop.

The restaurants and coffee shops listed here allow one well-behaved dog at the time of this printing. If you have more than one dog that you would like to bring with you, definitely contact the management and see if it's okay.

SAN DIEGO

Berta's Latin American
3928 Twiggs Street
Old Town
(619) 295-2343
Make reservations for your dog.

Caffe Italia
1704 India Street
Little Italy
(619) 234-6767

Downtown Johnny Brown's
1220 3rd Avenue
Downtown
(619) 232-8414

Froglander's Yogurt
6027 Paseo Delicias # H
Rancho Santa Fe
(858) 756-3764

Girard Gourmet
7837 Girard Road
La Jolla
(619) 454-3321

Hard Rock Cafe
801 4th Avenue
Gaslamp District
(619) 615-7625

K-9 Country Club
202 'C' Street
Downtown
(619) 239-0304

La Terrazza
8008 Girard Avenue
La Jolla
(858) 459-9750

Living Room Coffee House
5987 El Cajon Boulevard
College Area
(619) 287-8186

Living Room Coffee House
1417 University Road
Hillcrest
(619) 295-7911

Living Room Coffee House
1010 Prospect Street
La Jolla
(858) 459-1187

Point Loma Seafood
2805 Emerson Street
Point Loma
(619) 223-1109

Rebecca's
3023 Juniper Street
North Park
(619) 284-3663

Red's Cafe
1021 Rosecrans
Point Loma
(619) 523-5540

Roppongo
875 Prospect Street
La Jolla
(858) 551-5252

Rubio's Baja Grill
901 4th Avenue, Gaslamp District
(619) 231-7731

Rudy's Café at the Shores
2168 Avenida De La Playa
La Jolla Shores
(858) 454-5665

Sally's Restaurant & Bar
1 Market Place, Seaport Village
(619) 687-6080

Sammy's California Woodfired Pizza
770 4th Avenue
Gaslamp District
(619) 230-8888

Before going to a restaurant or coffee shop, make sure your dog relieves itself. It would be disrespectful to other patrons if your dog went to the bathroom while they were trying to eat.

©Casey Orr

Never leave your dog alone at a table.

©Casey Orr

Shelby's
6737 La Jolla Boulevard
La Jolla
(858) 456-6660

Sidewalk Café at the Grant Hotel
326 Broadway
Downtown
(619) 232-3121

Terra
1270 Cleveland Avenue
Hillcrest
(619) 293-7088

The Galley at Pirates Cave
712 Garnet Avenue
Pacific Beach
(858) 274-7427

Trattoria La Strada
702 5th Avenue
Gaslamp District
(619) 239-3400
Call for reservations for your dog.

Trattoria Portobello
715 4th Avenue
Gaslamp District
(619) 232-4440

Twiggs Coffee House
4590 Park Boulevard
University Heights
(619) 296-0616

Westgate Gourmet at The Westgate
1055 2nd Avenue
San Diego
(619) 557-3698

SOLANA BEACH

Sushi Station
125 N. Highway 101
(619) 481-9800

NOTES

NOTES

Chapter Seven

©Casey Orr

Hotels & Motels

Hotels & Motels

If you are trying to find a pet-friendly hotel for a guest coming to San Diego, or simply need one yourself, you'll find you have much to choose from. Everything from luxury hotels to simple chain motels are readily available for traveling pet lovers.

©Casey Orr

Your choices depend on your needs and your budget: some motels offer only basic amenities - a bed for you, an area for you to walk your dog and not much else except a reasonable price. If you require a bit more pampering, we have found wonderful dog-friendly places that have complete packages that cover your needs. These packages can include a room complete with leashes, soft doggie beds, water dishes, complimentary dog biscuits - even pet room service with specialize service!

Don't expect to just waltz in with your dog though - most require reservations. Some motels have size/weight restrictions for your pooch and some will tack on an added fee for each pet. Many require a deposit that will be refunded to you as you leave, so make sure you call first and find out their requirements.

Who wants to travel without their best buddy? We'll make it easy for you listing the places within the County that will ensure your comfort and meet your needs, and that will make traveling with your dog a worry-free and comfortable experience.

CARLSBAD

Inns of America
751 Raintree Drive
(760) 931-1185
Additional $10/day.

Motel 6
1006 Carlsbad Village Drive
(760) 434-7135

Motel 6
6117 Paseo Del Norte
(760) 438-1242

Motel 6
750 Raintree Drive
(760) 431-0745

CHULA VISTA

La Quinta Inn
150 Bonita Road
(619) 691-1211
Dogs 40 lbs. or less.

Motel 6
745 'E' Street
(619) 422-4200
Dogs 30 lbs. or less.

Vagabond Inn
230 Broadway
(619) 422-8305
Additional $10/day.

CORONADO

Crown City Inn
520 Orange Avenue
(619) 435-3116

Loews Coronado Bay Resort
4000 Coronado Bay Road
(619) 424-4000

Even if the hotel or motel is dog-friendly, ask the management if it's okay to bring your dog into lobby area. Some hotels or motels may not want to inconvenience other patrons or make them feel uncomfortable by allowing dogs in a common area.

When staying in a hotel room with your dog, place the "Do Not Disturb" on the door to avoid housekeeping from entering the room. Your dog may think housekeeping is an intruder and become protective in aggressive manner.

DEL MAR

Clarion
720 Camino Del Mar
(858) 755-0765
Off-season only. $25 nonrefundable cleaning fee.

EL CAJON

Best Western Courtesy Inn
1355 E. Main Street
(800) 528-1234
Additional $6/day.

Budget Host Hacienda
588 N. Mollison Avenue
(800) 283-4678

Motel 6
550 Montrose Court
(619) 588-6100

ENCINITAS

Best Western
85 Encinitas Boulevard
(800) 528-1234
$50 nonreturnable cleaning fee.

Econo Lodge
410 N. Coast Highway
(619) 436-4999
Dogs 10 lbs. or less.

ESCONDIDO

Castle Creek Inn Resort & Spa
29850 Circle "R" Way
(800) 253-5341
$100 refundable deposit plus additional $10/day.

Lawrence Welk Resort
8860 Lawrence Welk Drive
(800) 932-9355
$25 nonrefundable cleaning charge.

Motel 6
900 N. Quince Street
(760) 745-9252
Dogs 20 lbs. or smaller.

LA MESA

Motel 6
7621 Alvarado Road
(619) 469-3172
One dog per room.

NATIONAL CITY

Holiday Inn-South Bay
700 National City Boulevard
(800) 465-4329

Red Lion Inn & Suites
801 National City Boulevard
(619) 336-1100
$25 refundable deposit.

OCEANSIDE

Motel 6
3708 Plaza Drive
(760) 941-1011
One dog per room.

POWAY

Poway Country Inn
13845 Poway Road
(800) 648-6320

RAMONA

Ramona Valley Inn
416 Main Street
(800) 648-4618
Dogs 20 lbs. or less.

Rancho Bernardo

La Quinta Motor Inn
10185 Paseo Montril
(800) 531-5900
Dogs 25 lbs. or less.

Never leave your dog alone in the hotel or motel room. This is a very unfamiliar place for your pooch and he or she may be scared or stressed by being alone. He or she may retaliate by destroying furniture or disrupt neighbors by excessive barking.

©Casey Orr

When traveling with your dog, make sure to pack for your dog as well. Your doggie traveling pack should include:

- *Two bowls, one for food, the other for water.*
- *Dog food and treats.*
- *A leash.*
- *Your dog's bed and blanket.*
- *Your dog's favorite toy.*
- *Bags.*
- *First Aid kit.*

Residence Inn by Marriott
11002 Rancho Carmel Drive
(800) 331-3131
$150 nonreturnable cleaning fee plus additional $10/day.

Travelodge
16929 W. Bernardo Drive
(800) 578-7878

RANCHO SANTA FE

Inn at Rancho Santa Fe
5951 Linea del Cielo
(800) 654-2928

SAN DIEGO

Beach Haven Inn
4740 Mission Boulevard
(800) 831-6323
Dogs 20 lbs. or less.

Best Western Lamplighter Inn & Suites
6474 El Cajon Boulevard
(800) 545-0778
Additional $10/day.

Crown Point View Suite Hotel
4088 Crown Point Drive
(800) 338-3331

Diamond Head Inn
605 Diamond Street
(858) 273-1900
$30 nonrefundable cleaning fee.

Doubletree Hotel-Mission Valley
7450 Hazard Center Drive
(619) 297-5466

Econo Lodge-San Diego By The Bay
1655 Pacific Highway
(800) 424-4777
Small dogs.

Holiday Inn on The Bay
1355 N. Harbor Drive
(800) 877-8920

Homestead Village
7444 Mission Valley Road
(619) 299-2292
$75 nonreturnable cleaning fee.

Marriott Hotel
4240 La Jolla Village Drive
(800) 228-9290
$50 nonrefundable cleaning fee.

Marriott Hotel & Marina San Diego
333 West Harbor Drive
(800) 228-9290
Small dogs. $50 nonreturnable cleaning fee.

Marriott Suites-Downtown
701 "A' Street
(800) 962-1367
Small dogs. $50 nonrefundable cleaning fee.

Motel 6 - Hotel Circle
2424 Hotel Circle N.
(619) 296-1612

Motel 6 - North
5592 Clairemont Mesa Boulevard
(858) 268-9758

Pacific Shores Inn
4802 Mission Boulevard
(800) 826-0715
Dogs 50 lbs. or less. $35 nonreturnable cleaning fee.

Radisson Hotel-San Diego
1433 Camino Del Rio
(800) 333-3333
Dogs 35 lbs. or lesser. $50 refundable deposit.

©Casey Orr

When taking your dog out to eliminate waste, make sure it's away from other hotel rooms or common areas as a courtesy to other visitors. And always make sure you bring a bag to pick up your dog's waste and discard it properly.

Always keep an eye on your dog. Beware of children running up to your pooch putting your dog on the defense. What may seem innocent on a child's part may be taken as aggressive to your dog.

Red Lion Hanalei Hotel
2270 Hotel Circle North
(800) 882-0858
Dogs 50 lbs. or less. $50 refundable deposit.

Residence Inn by Marriott
8901 Gilman Drive
(800) 331-3131

Residence Inn by Marriott Kearny Mesa
5400 Kearny Mesa Road
(800) 331-3131
$100 nonrefundable cleaning fee. Additional $7/day.

San Diego Marriott Mission Valley
8757 Rio San Diego Drive
(800) 228-9290
$150 refundable deposit plus $50 nonreturnable cleaning fee.

San Diego Mission Valley Hilton
901 Camino Del Rio
(800) 445-8667
Dogs 30 lbs. or smaller. $175 refundable deposit.

U.S. Grant Hotel
326 Broadway
(800) 237-5029

Vagabond Inn - Airport
1655 Pacific Highway
(619) 232-6391
Additional $10/day.

Vagabond Inn - Mission Valley
625 Hotel Circle South
(800) 522-1555
Additional $10/day.

Vagabond Inn - Point Loma
1325 Scott Street
(619) 422-8305
Additional $10/day.

Vagabond Inn - San Diego
4540 Mission Bay Drive
(858) 274-7888
Additional $10/day.

SAN MARCOS

Quails Inn at Lake San Marcos
1025 La Bonita Drive
(760) 744-0120

SAN YSIDRO

International Motor Inn
190 E. Calle Primera
(619) 428-4486
Small dogs.

Motel 6
160 E. Calle Primera
(619) 690-6663

SOLANA BEACH

Holiday Inn
621 S. Highway 101
(858) 350-0111

VISTA

La Quinta Inn
630 Sycamore Avenue
(760) 727-8180

©*Casey Orr*

Ask your concierge where the closest dog park or park that allows dogs is. Discover that park and explore the community with your dog. You may be amazed by what the two of you may find.

NOTES

Chapter Eight

Boarding, Daycare & Pet Sitting

Boarding, Daycare & Pet Sitting

©Casey Orr

There are many reasons to board your pet. You might have a family emergency that requires you to quickly leave home. You may be a working owner with a bored pet who would benefit from some regular socialization. Or you may have planned an overseas vacation and simply can't bring your pet. All of these needs require a unique solution - would you know which to choose?

For the pet left home day after day, a doggie daycare might be the perfect solution. This is a facility that provides care, socialization and even training of dogs for a day at a time. As pet owner, you can drop your dog off in the morning and pick him up at the end of the day. Don't have time in the morning? Some of them even offer shuttle services.

In a similar vein, there are kennels that will care for your dog for longer periods. Both of these types of places provide a healthy, safe, and fun environment for you pet.

If you have a pet that is more comfortable in his own home, you can choose a pet sitter. You can have a sitter stay on premises and care for your home as well as your dog. Alternatively, they will come over once or twice a day just to feed, play with, and ensure your dogs needs are taken care of.

If you decide to board your pet, you'll certainly want to find the most comfortable accommodations possible in a place where you can be certain your dog is well-treated.

A good daycare, kennel, or pet-sitter will strive to provide a fun environment for your pet, and the staff should actively enjoy dogs. In the next chapter, we'll list the options available in San Diego.

All of the places listed should be contacted for more information. As any responsible dog owner knows, carefully check references for anyone or organization you are trusting your dog with. Jane's Dog Guide does not endorse any particular individual or organization. It is YOUR responsibility to make an informed decision.

Boarding

BONITA

Jensen's Kennel
3655 Proctor Valley Road
(619) 479-7074

Sweetwater Valley Animal Inn
5540 San Miguel Road
(619) 479-4791

BONSALL

Bonsall Veterinary Clinic
6009 West Lilac Road
(760) 724-7186

CARLSBAD

Mohnacky Animal Hospital
2505 S. Vista Way
(760) 729-3330
www.vet.com

Pacific Coast K-9's Seacrest
7250 Ponto Drive
(760) 438-2469

EL CAJON

Blossom Valley Groom & Board
9400 Blossom Valley Road
(619) 443-4271

Canine Sports Center
4821 Dehesa Road
(619) 588-4821

Cricket Ridge Kennels
1329 E. Chase
(619) 447-8020

Rancho San Diego Animal Hospital
2988 Jamacha Road
(619) 660-6767

Look for these things when visiting a boarding or daycare facility prior to making a decision:

- *An attentive staff.*
- *Adequate number of staff members.*
- *Clean conditions.*
- *Waste picked up immediately.*
- *Ample space for dogs to rest and play.*
- *No overcrowding.*
- *Safe environment.*

A benefit of boarding and daycare facilities is that your dog will be in a constant social environment. Dogs need human companionship, attention and communication and these places can provide that 24 hours.

©Casey Orr

ENCINITAS

Alcala Pet Care
1273 Crest Drive
(760) 436-6619
www.alcalapetcare.com

Animal Keeper The
155 Saxony Road
(760) 753-9366
www.animalkeeper.com

Drake Center for Animal Health
195 N. El Camino Real
(760) 753-9393

Holiday Pet Hotel & Cat's Pajamas
551 Union Street
(760) 753-6754
www.holidaypethotel.com

Point Loma Pomeranians
1726 Crest Drive
(760) 753-5807

ESCONDIDO

Absolute K9 Training
PO Box 301637
(800) 889-3647
www.absolutek9.com

Acacia Animal Hospital
1040 North Broadway
(760) 745-8115
www.acaciavet.com

FALLBROOK

Fallbrook Animal Lodge
1115 E. Mission Road
(760) 728-0892

LA MESA

Fuerte Animal Hospital
4670 Avocado Boulevard
(619) 440-1432

La Mesa Pet Hotel
8126 Center Street
(619) 466-6166
www.lamesa-pethotel.com

Lake Murray Village Veterinary
5644 Lake Murray Boulevard
(619) 464-3177

LAKESIDE

Carter Kennels
8755 Winter Gardens Boulevard
(619) 561-7464

County Kennels
16922 Rio Maria Road
(858) 748-5771

Greywood Kennels
9078 Winter Gardens Boulevard
(619) 443-7605

Kennedy Kennels
8934 Creekford Drive
(619) 443-8687

LEMON GROVE

San Diego Pet Hospital
7368 Broadway
(619) 462-6600

NORTH COUNTY

Pet Care Services
(760) 432-9750

OCEANSIDE

Animal Keeper The
3532 College Boulevard
(760) 941-3221
www.animalkeeper.com

Mohnacky Animal Hospital
3504-E College Boulevard
(760) 945-1000
www.vet.com

©Casey Orr

"Strays and animals rescued from the pound/shelter make the best pets. They know you saved their lives and are eternally grateful. In reality, we are the grateful ones. We have a best friend for life, who will love us no matter what. And we will love them right back."

Emily and Gus Rios
Prieta - chow/lab mix,
Whitey - shepherd mix,
Sticks - chow/shepherd mix,
Caesar - lab/pit mix
College area

If your dog seems scared or uncomfortable about going to daycare, your dog may be mishandled. Talk to the owner and ask how they handle their dogs in different situations. If their methods are not gentle or to your liking, find another daycare facility or option for the sake of your dog.

©Casey Orr

Oceanside Pet Hotel & Training
2909 San Luis Rey Road
(760) 757-2345
www.go.to/OPH

Temple Heights Animal Hospital
4750 Oceanside Boulevard
(760) 630-3590

POWAY

Animal Keeper The
12280 Oak Knoll Road
(858) 748-9676
www.animalkeeper.com

Royal Serchek Samoyed Kennel
14950 Garden Road
(858) 748-3191

RAMONA

Animal Artistry's Grooming & Boarding
202 6th Street
(760) 789-7436

Kritter Kamp
25155 Creek Hollow Drive
(760) 788-6799

RANCHO SANTA FE

Club Pet Boarding Center – Helen Woodward Animal Center
6525 Calle Del Nido
(858) 756-4117

SAN DIEGO

AAA Pet Care
(619) 579-8301

Airport Pet Resort
246 W. Washington
(619) 299-7388

Arena Animal Hospital Grooming &
3625 Midway Drive
(619) 223-2166

Best Friends Pet Resort & Salon
8020 Ronson Road
(858) 565-8055
www.bestfriendspetcare.com

Cabrillo Pet Care Center
4130 Voltaire Street
(619) 224-9516

Camp Diego
2926 Garnet Avenue
(619) 224-9516

Center Veterinary Clinic
8963 Mira Mesa Boulevard
(858) 271-1152

Fon Jon Kennels
5050 Santa Fe Street
(858) 273-2266

Golden Paw, The
5305 Metro Street
(619) 299-2730
www.thegoldenpaw.com

La Jolla Pet Resort
7520 Fay Avenue
(858) 454-6155

Markim Pet Resort
(858) 481-3881

Morena Pet Hospital & Bird Center
1540 Morena Boulevard
(619) 275-0888

Pacific Beach Kennels
1964 Garnet Avenue
(858) 274-8844

Pink Poodle Pet Salon
6134 El Cajon Boulevard
(619) 583-8861

©Casey Orr

In order to prevent your dog from contracting diseases from other dogs, keep your dog up-to-date with their vaccinations, worming and flea and tick treatment.

©Casey Orr

Ask the daycare facility if they perform a behavior/temperament evaluation of the dogs that stay there. You want to make sure that all dogs will be friendly and that there aren't any bullies in daycare.

VCA Hillcrest Animal Center
246 W. Washington Street
(619) 299-7387
www.vca.com

SAN MARCOS

Animal Care Center
330 Rancheros Drive
(760) 471-2873

California School of Dog Grooming
655 S. Rancho Santa Fe Road
(760) 471-0787

Levitt Animal Hospital
1155 Grand Avenue
(760) 744-5242

Mohnacky Animal Hospital
997 W. San Marcos Boulevard
(760) 744-0032
www.vet.com

Palomar Animal Hospital
2615 S. Santa Fe Avenue
(760) 727-7622

Paw-Dre's Clubhouse for Pets
1049 E. Mission Road
(760) 745-2759
www.sdco-op.com/pets

San Marcos Training & Boarding
130 S. Twin Oaks Valley Road
(760) 744-5171

SANTEE

Rose Hill Kennels
8756 Cottonwood Avenue
(619) 448-9071

S U - E T S Kennels - Scottish Terriers
10631 Prospect Avenue
(619) 448-8760

SOLANA BEACH

Rancho-Solana Pet Spa
247 S. Highway 101
(858) 755-9318

SOUTH BAY

For Paws Pet Care
(619) 283-7387

SPRING VALLEY

Bark Park
3971 Spring Drive
(619) 461-5577

Jay Bee's Kennel
9124 Olive Drive
(619) 463-2573

Spring Creek Kennel & Cattery
9279 Campo Road
(619) 463-1722

VALLEY CENTER

Alibi Acres Kennels
16750 Paradise Mountain Road
(760) 749-4100

VISTA

Brengle Terrace Animal Hospital
971 Vale Terrace Drive
(760) 724-7186

Canine Castle Dog Boarding
814 Crest View Road
(760) 726-2068
www.caninecastle.com

Ce Ce Belle Pet Hotel
29920 Margate Lane
(760) 758-7322 • www.sharbelle.com

Margale Kennels
29976 Margale Lane
(760) 726-3391

Bring these things when taking your dog to a boarding and daycare facility:

- *Vaccinations records*
- *Emergency contact information*
- *Your veterinarian's phone number and address*
- *Special instructions for medication, feeding, grooming and other care*
- *Your dog's favorite toy*

©Casey Orr

"I love to watch my dogs sleep."

Monica Bahr
Lily
San Diego

Melrose Veterinary Hospital
1680 S. Melrose Drive
(760) 727-5151

Tri-City Veterinary Clinic
1929 W. Vista Way
(760) 758-2091

Vista Veterinary Hospital
1139 S. Santa Fe Avenue
(760) 726-1234

Daycare

CARLSBAD

Mohnacky Animal Hospital
2505 S. Vista Way
(760) 729-3330
www.vet.com

Pets in Paradise
(760) 942-7387

NORTH COUNTY

Day Care for Dogs
(858) 481-8922

OCEANSIDE

Mohnacky Animal Hospital
3504-E College Boulevard
(760) 945-1000
www.vet.com

Oceanside Pet Hotel & Training
2909 San Luis Rey Road
(760) 757-2345
www.go.to/OPH

SAN DIEGO

Best Friends Pet Resort & Salon
8020 Ronson Road
(858) 565-8055
www.bestfriendspetcare.com

Camp Diego
2926 Garnet Avenue
(619) 224-9516

Markim Pet Resort
(858) 481-3881

Mission Valley Kennels
4325 Twain Avenue
(619) 282-0022

Pacific Beach Kennels
1964 Garnet Avenue
(858) 274-8844

The Golden Paw Pet Resort
5305 Metro Street
(619) 299-2730
www.TheGoldenPaw.net

SAN MARCOS

Mohnacky Animal Hospital
997 W. San Marcos Boulevard
(760) 744-0032
www.vet.com

Paw-Dre's Clubhouse for Pets
1049 E. Mission Road
(760) 745-2759 • www.sdco-op.com/pets

SOUTH BAY

For Paws Pet Care
South Bay
(619) 283-7387

SPRING VALLEY

Spring Valley
3971 Spring Drive
(619) 461-5577

VISTA

Canine Castle Dog Boarding
814 Crest View Road
(760) 726-2068
www.caninecastle.com

If you are going to be away for a while and a pet sitter will be watching your dog, make sure you buy enough food and supplies for the duration.

Pet Sitting

The benefits of pet sitting for your dog are:

- *No exposure to other animals and diseases.*
- *Remains in his or her familiar environment.*
- *Gets to eat his or her regular food.*
- *Can maintain a routine exercise schedule.*
- *No drop-off hassle.*

ALPINE

Alpine Pet Sitters
(619) 445-3920

CARDIFF BY THE SEA

Being There Pet Sitting
(760) 942-8880

CARLSBAD

Petcetera
Carlsbad, Encinitas
(760) 730-9697

Petpurri Pet Care
(760) 434-3283

DEL MAR

Del Mar Pet Sitter Service
(858) 793-9590

Menagerie Minders in Home Pet
(858) 481-2253

EAST COUNTY

Margo's Paw Tenders
(619) 460-2286

Pet Sitting by Trish
Lemon Grove, La Mesa, College
(619) 283-7624

Sylvia's Pet Sitting & Home Care
Spring Valley, La Mesa, El Cajon
(619) 475-7612

ENCINITAS

Pet Watchers Plus
(760) 943-1745

TLC Pet Care
(760) 942-6500

FALLBROOK

On Call Services
(760) 723-3445

Paws and Claws Pet Sitting
Fallbrook Area
(760) 731-1418

NORTH COUNTY

Always Reliable Pet Care
(760) 489-1437

Angel Pet Care
(760) 597-1606

Annette's Pet Sitting
(760) 747-1944

Anytime Pet Sitting
(760) 480-5570

Auntie Jan's Pet & House Sitting
(760) 602-7882

Columbo's Critter Care
(760) 432-6826

Country Pet Sitting Service
(760) 787-0892

Creature Comfort Pet Sitting
(760) 744-4984

Diamond Development
(760) 720-7387

Doggie Daze Daycare
(760) 631-7297

Five Star Pet Care
(858) 451-9129

Gotta Lovett
(760) 631-1101
www.gottalovettpetsitting.com

Many boarding kennels provide on-site training. Take advantage of this next time you go out of town and put your dog through a training program while being boarded. It will cost more but may be well worth it.

Make sure that where ever your dog is going to stay, there is plenty of fresh air and shade for them to play and rest in. San Diego is arid and the heat can be dangerous to your dog.

Home Alone Pet Sitting Service
(760) 746-8144

Home'n'Happy Pet Care
(760) 724-1686

Hometenders
(760) 728-5000

Jamie's Pet Sitting
(760) 746-2065

K-9s, Kitties & Kritters
(760) 747-1041

Marybear Pet Sitting Services
La Jolla, University Towne
(858) 272-6425

P.A.W.S. - Paula's Animal Watching
(760) 533-7297

Pat's Pet Sitting
(760) 727-0558

Paws at Home
(858) 674-4982

Pawsatively 4 Pets
(760) 735-8465

Pet Care Services
(760) 432-9750

Pet Guardian Professional Pet
(760) 736-1918

Pet Nanny
(760) 439-9690

Pet Sitters of North County
(760) 941-5471

Pet Sitting by DeAnne
(858) 748-4679

Pet-Tenders
North County
(760) 727-6816
www.pet-tenders.com

Poway-Bernardo Pet Sitting
Poway and Rancho Bernardo
(858) 748-3441

Preferred Pet Care
(760) 233-7423

Priority Home Pet Care
(760) 720-0173

Two Paws Up
(760) 749-4022

While Away - Professional Pet Sitting
(619) 855-7387

NORTH COUNTY INLAND

Kim Kare Pet Sitting Service
(858) 538-9353

Mrs. Doolittle Pet & Housesitters
(760) 727-6894
www.angelfire.com/ca4/mrsdoolittle

OCEANSIDE

Able Pet Sitting
(760) 754-1988

Classy Clips
(760) 721-1562

Kompanion Kare Pet Sitting
(760) 736-0330

Wagtime Pet Sitting
(760) 433-1080

RAMONA

Karen's Critter Care
(760) 788-5494

Some boarding and daycare facilities offer pick-up and delivery services, not only from and to your home, but also to and from your vet and groomer.

By having boarding/sitting options available to you, you may be saving a friendship by not imposing on a friend's busy schedule.

SAN DIEGO

A Guardian Angel's Pet Care
(619) 298-4818

A-1 Pet Sitter Referral Service
(619) 298-6446

All My Furry Friends
Pacific Beach
(858) 272-8422

Animal Amigo's
(858) 653-3808

Animals R Us
Pacific Beach, La Jolla
(858) 483-7387

Aunt Sally's Pet Sitting Service
(858) 270-0837
http://home.san.rr.com/auntsandy

Beach N Bay Pet Sitting
Pacific Beach, Point Loma
(858) 922-2683

Canine Cleaners
(858) 503-6727

Critter Sitter - Deborah Loving
(858) 756-9635

Crystal's Pet Sitting of La Jolla
(858) 456-3930

Dac's House & Pet Sitting
(619) 583-2885

Diane's Pet Care
(619) 298-6112

For Paws Pet Care & Boarding
(619) 283-7387

For Pete's Sake
(619) 284-5656

Fuzzie Friendz Pet & House
(619) 298-4818

Home Sitting Seniors
(619) 280-4080

Honeydo
(858) 270-4764

House Sitters International
(619) 469-5700

Jennifer's Pet Sitting
N. County Inland
(858) 566-6112

Jewel's Pet Sitting
(858) 272-9771

Joanne's Petsitting & House
(619) 465-3512

La Jolla Pet Sitting
(858) 581-2076

Little Guy's Pet Sitting
Pacific Beach, Point Loma, Ocean Beach
(858) 274-5076

Liz's Pet Care & Dog Walking
(858) 569-1370

Love and Care Pet Sitters
(619) 231-3116
www.loveandcarepetsitters.com

Love Your Pets
(619) 758-9231

Margo's Paw Tenders
(619) 460-2287

No Place Like Home
Clairemont, Bay Park
(619) 222-9644

©Casey Orr

Many pet sitters offer services other than just taking care of your pooch, such as turning on and off your lights for home security purposes, bringing in your mail and newspapers, bringing out your garbage to the curb on trash day and watering your plants. Ask your pet sitter next time you go out of town.

For peace of mind, don't hesitate to call the boarding kennel, daycare facility or pet sitter to get an update on your best friend. Most places want you to be at ease as well as your return patronage.

No Sad Tails Pet Sitting
(619) 390-1381

Noah's Ark Pet Sitting Service
(858) 273-2660

Ocean Beach Pet Sitting
(619) 224-0722

Original Paw Pleasers, The
Hillcrest
(619) 293-7297
www.pawpleasers.com

Pat Loves Pets Animal Care
North County
(858) 513-6532

Pawprints In-home Pet Sitting
(619) 624-0360

Peninsula Pet Valet
(619) 224-4475

Pet Butler
(619) 286-6263

Pet Granny 92103
(619) 297-7387

Pet Lover Professional Pet Sitting
La Jolla
(619) 501-3506

Pet Loving Care
La Jolla, Del Mar
(858) 337-1992

Pet Pals In-Home Pet Sitting
(858) 456-1827
www.petpals-petsitting.com

Pet Passion Pet Sitting
Central San Diego
(858) 270-0552

Pet Sitter's Association
(888) 473-8748

Pet TLC
Golden Hill, Downtown, Coronado
(619) 544-0130

Pet-Tenders
(619) 298-3033
www.pet-tenders.com

Purrfect Pet Sitting
Normal Heights, Kensington
(619) 528-0218

Sandy's Animal Services
Clairemont & surrounding areas
(858) 273-6022

Spoil ' em Rotten Pet Sitting
Large Area of San Diego
(619) 595-9974
www.spoilemrottenpetsitting.com

Vicki's Pampered Pet Care
(619) 583-0730
www.veternet.com/vicki.html

Wags & Whiskers Loving Pet Care
(619) 226-0722

Wags to Purrs
Scripps Ranch
(858) 695-0940

While Away - Professional Pet Sitting
(619) 955-7387

SANTEE

Santee Pet Sitting
Santee, San Carlos
(619) 449-7165

Always be a responsible dog owner and check for references. Your dog is depending on you.

Call the Pet Sitters Association at (888) 473-8748 for referrals.

SOUTH BAY

For Paws Pet Care
(619) 283-7387

Spoil Me Rotten
Chula Vista, Bonita
(619) 426-3753

SPRING VALLEY

Jay Bee's Kennel
(619) 463-2573

NOTES

NOTES

Chapter Nine

Veterinary Hospitals & Clinics

Veterinary Hospitals & Clinics

Your veterinarian will be with you for a long time, and it may be one of the most important relationships you and your dog will have. It's crucial that you choose your vet wisely. It goes without saying that your vet should have the appropriate certifications, but it also important to find somebody you can trust, and who understands the importance of your relationship with your animal companion.

There are other considerations as well. You'll need to pay attention to the office location, hours of service, friendliness of staff, and commitment of doctors. Fees are important, and you must know how emergencies are handled.

In this next chapter, we'll teach you what to look for when choosing your veterinarian, and give you a list of things to consider when making this important choice. We'll also give you an overview of vaccination schedules and routine health care for your dog. We will demystify the spaying/neutering issue and help you make an informed decision.

While we will not endorse any one veterinarian or clinic here, in this chapter we will list major clinics and emergency centers only. To find a veterinarian in your area that may be in private practice, consult the San Diego County Veterinarian Society at 619-640-9583, and ALWAYS check references. They can you help to make an informed decision on who and where you should take your dog. Your best friend deserves the finest care possible so take your time and choose wisely.

Emergency Clinics

CHULA VISTA

South County Emergency Animal Clinic
3438 Bonita Road
(619) 427-2881

DEL MAR

Animal & Bird Hospital
2132 Jimmy Durante Boulevard
(858) 755-9351

ESCONDIDO

Escondido Veterinary Urgent Care
2525 South Centre City Parkway
(760) 738-9600

LA MESA

A Pet Emergency & Specialty Center
5232 Jackson Drive
(619) 462-4800

SAN DIEGO

Animal Emergency Clinic
13240 Evening Creek Drive
(858) 748-7387

Animal ER of San Diego
5610 Kearny Mesa Road, Suite B
(858) 596-0600

Emergency Animal Hospital & Referral Center
2317 Hotel Circle South
(619) 299-2400

SAN MARCOS

North County Emergency Animal
100 B Rancho Santa Fe Rd Suite 133
(760) 734-4433

"You should spay or neuter your dog before six months of age. A female dog should be spayed before the onset of estrus. By neutering your pup, you will not only get a year free on your dog license, but your pet will gain lifelong well-being and happiness. Sterilized pets lead safer, healthier lives. Neutering your male will stop the tendency to roam becoming lost and getting into fights. Spaying a female eliminates the risk of certain cancers. It's not only better for your pet, but also better for the community. Also, neutering at almost 6 months allows for the baby teeth to be removed if they are retained."

Dr. John Hetzler, DVM
Ark Animal Hospital

Veterinarian Clinics

ALPINE

Alpine Veterinary Clinic
2113 Arnold Way
(619) 445-6262

BONITA

Town & Country Animal Hospital
4055 Bonita Road
(619) 479-3311

BONSALL

Bonsall Pet Hospital
5519 Mission Road, Suite H
(760) 630-1711

BRAWLEY

Brawley Animal Clinic
266 West Highway 86
(760) 344-3531

Howard Veterinary Consultation
PO Box 191
(760) 344-5738

Mange should be checked out by your veterinarian since there are many different types of mites that can cause it. A veterinarian will be able to determine the type and treat it accordingly.

CARDIFF BY THE SEA

Cardiff Animal Hospital, Inc.
2159 San Elijo Avenue
(760) 436-3215

CARLSBAD

Aardvark Animal Health Center
6986 El Camino Real
(760) 438-7766

Carlsbad Animal Clinic
2739 State Street
(760) 729-4431

Mohnacky Animal Hospital
2505 S. Vista Way
(760) 729-3330

CHULA VISTA

A Cat & Dog Emergency
3438 Bonita Road
(619) 427-2233

Amazon Animal Hospital
1172 3rd Avenue, Suite D-8
(619) 476-0053

Bonita Mountain Road Pet Clinic & Hospital
3438 Bonita Road
(619) 427-2233

Eastlake Village Veterinary Clinic
2260 Otay Lakes Road, Suite 113
(619) 482-9100

Melrose Pet Clinic
1466 Melrose Avenue
(619) 427-2851

Otay Lakes Veterinary Clinic
736 Otay Lakes Road
(619) 482-2000

Pet Clinic, The
3326 Main Street
(619) 422-0194

South Bay Veterinary Clinic
1038 Broadway
(619) 422-6186

South County Emergency Animal
3438 Bonita Road
(619) 427-2881

Third Avenue Animal Medical Center
1280 3rd Avenue
(619) 420-6423

Vetsmart Veterinary Hospital
820 Paseo De Rey
(619) 656-1928

"Some dogs eat twice a day, others only once. It really depends on the dog's preference as well as your own. Dogs do like to eat with each other and with you and your family. Eating at the same time as everyone else reaffirms their role in the pack, which provides a source of comfort for a dog and decreases appetite cravings."

Dr. John Hetzler, DVM
Ark Animal Hospital

"A puppy under a year will see the vet four or five times the first year. These visits will include the proper initial vaccines as well as provide early identification of any potential health problems. Adult dogs, providing there are no obvious health problems, should see the vet at least once per year.

Elderly dogs should see the vet at least 2 times per year, more often if chronic health problems exist."

Dr. John Hetzler, DVM
Ark Animal Hospital

CORONADO

Coronado Veterinary Hospital
150 Orange Avenue
(619) 435-6281

Crown Veterinary Hospital
817 Orange Avenue
(619) 435-6624

DEL MAR

All Creatures Hospital
3665 Via De La Valle
(858) 481-7992

Animal and Bird Hospital of Del Mar
2132 Jimmy Durante Boulevard
(858) 755-9351

EL CAJON

Abbey Clinic for Pets
1787 E. Main Street
(619) 442-8300

ABC Veterinary Hospital of El Cajon
522 E. Chase Avenue
(619) 590-6160

Animal Care Clinic
2650 Jamacha Road, Suite 159
(619) 670-8700

Broadway Animal Hospital
380 Broadway Street
(619) 444-1166

Cajon Rancho Pet Hospital
1682 Greenfield Drive
(619) 442-5571

El Cajon Valley Veterinary Hospital
560 N. Johnson Avenue
(619) 444-9491

Jamacha Veterinary Clinic
693 Jamacha Road
(619) 579-0377

Judy Veterinary Clinic
1764 N. Second Avenue
(619) 449-3500

Rancho San Diego Animal Hospital
2988 Jamacha Road
(619) 660-6767

Valhalla Veterinary Clinic
1498 Jamacha Road, Suite 104
(619) 440-4747

Vetsmart Veterinary Hospital
865 Jackman Street
(858) 401-0387

ENCINITAS

Drake Center For Animal Care, The
195 N. El Camino Real
(760) 753-9393

Santa Fe Animal Hospital
301 Santa Fe Drive
(760) 753-6512

Village Square Animal Hospital
1466 Encinitas Boulevard
(760) 942-1220

ESCONDIDO

Aark Animal Hospital
1326 W. Mission Road
(760) 745-1108

Acacia Animal Hospital
1040 North Broadway
(760) 745-8115

Animal Medical Hospital of
130 North Hale Avenue
(760) 741-8221

"Normal temperature for dogs ranges from 101.5 to 102.5. You can take your dog's temperature rectally using an electronic thermometer with a disposable end. These devices have become relatively inexpensive and most people with children already have them on hand."

Dr. John Hetzler, DVM
Ark Animal Hospital

If your dog has an upset stomach or diarrhea, allow him or her to skip a meal yet provide enough water so your dog doesn't dehydrate. When reintroducing food to your dog, serve bland foods and give her some Pepto Bismo to coat your dog's stomach. But always check with your veterinarian first to make sure if it's safe for your sick friend.

Companion Animal Clinic
1215 South Escondido Boulevard
(760) 743-2751

Escondido Veterinary Urgent Care
2525 S. Centre City Parkway
(760) 738-9600

Parkway Pet Clinic
855 E. Valley Parkway
(760) 743-0973

Veterinary Dermatology Services
2525 S. Centre City Parkway
(760) 480-9960

Veterinary Urgent Care Escondido
2525 S. Centre City Parkway
(760) 738-9600

Village Veterinary Hospital
316 W. Mission Avenue, Suite 113
(760) 741-9999

FALLBROOK

Alvarado Veterinary Hospital
347 East Alvarado
(760) 728-6606

Avocado Animal Hospital of Fallbrook
1111 East Mission Road
(760) 728-5771

IMPERIAL BEACH

Imperial Beach Pet Hospital
538 12th Street
(619) 424-3961

Seacoast Pet Clinic
600 Palm Avenue
(619) 429-7387

LA JOLLA

Animal Hospital of La Jolla
7601 Draper Avenue
(858) 459-2665

LA MESA

Cancer Treatment Center for Pets
9160 Fletcher Parkway
(619) 225-9684

Eastridge Veterinary Clinic
7750 University Avenue, Suite A
(619) 465-5291

El Cerrito Veterinary Hospital
6911 University Avenue
(619) 466-0533

Fuerte Animal Hospital
4670 Avocado Boulevard
(619) 440-1432

Helix Pet Hospital
4223 Palm Avenue
(619) 469-2129

La Mesa Pet Hospital
5336 Jackson Drive
(619) 469-0138

Lake Murray Animal Hospital
9029 Park Plaza Drive
(619) 461-5155

Lake Murray Village Veterinary
5644 Lake Murray Boulevard
(619) 464-3177

Parkway Pet Hospital
8200 Parkway Drive
(619) 463-9151

Pet Emergency & Specialty Center
5232 Jackson Drive, Suite 105
(619) 462-4800

When should I bring my dog to vet?

"You should obviously bring your dog to the vet when there is an accident or if there is protracted malaise. Dogs are good at hiding pain.

Malaise greater than 48 hours of onset should be considered emergent. For most eye problems wincing is a sign of discomfort and you dog needs to have a vet visit."

Dr. John Hetzler, DVM
Ark Animal Hospital

Ask your veterinarian for free first aid or poison charts that you can post on your frig or wall. It's always good to have emergency know-how readily available just in case of an accident.

Pet Emergency & Specialty Center
5232 Jackson Drive, Suite 105
(619) 462-4800

Rancho San Diego Village
3647 Avocado Boulevard
(619) 670-6278

University Animal Clinic
7134 University Avenue
(619) 463-9861

LAKESIDE

Lakeside Veterinary Hospital
9924 Maine Avenue
(619) 390-2342

Woodside Animal Hospital
12149 Woodside Avenue
(619) 561-5311

LEMON GROVE

Lemon Grove Veterinary Hospital
7572 North Avenue
(619) 463-0301

San Diego Pet Hospital
7368 Broadway
(619) 462-6600

NATIONAL CITY

Plaza Boulevard Pet Hospital
2415 E. Plaza Boulevard
(619) 267-8200

OCEANSIDE

Lone Star Veterinary Hospital
3870 Mission Avenue, Suite D-6
(760) 722-4840

Mohnacky Animal Hospital
3504-E College Boulevard
(760) 945-1000

Oceanside Veterinary Hospital
2960 San Luis Rey Road
(760) 757-1571

Pacific Animal Hospital
2801 Oceanside Boulevard
(760) 757-2442

Rancho Del Oro Animal Hospital
4093 Oceanside Boulevard, Suite J
(760) 945-0606

Temple Heights Animal Hospital
4750 Oceanside Boulevard
(760) 630-3590

POWAY

Midland Animal Clinic, Inc.
14210 Midland Road
(858) 566-0411

Poway Animal Hospital
12219 Poway Road
(858) 748-3326

RAMONA

Adobe Animal Hospital
1134 D Street
(760) 789-7090

Ramona Animal Hospital
1735 Main Street, Suite E
(760) 788-0960

Rancho Santa Fe
Criticare Veterinary Emergency
6525 Calle Del Nido
(858) 759-2255

Helen Woodward Animal Center
6461 El Apajo Road
(858) 756-4117

When your dog is pregnant, you may not notice any signs until the fifth week. Consult with your veterinarian if you see any signs of problems or pain.

If your dog gets a hot spot, trim the fur around the sore, clean it, apply an antiseptic recommended by your veterinarian and let it dry up to heal. And try to keep your dog from licking or scratching the hot spot.

Veterinary Specialty Hospital
6525 Calle Del Nido
(858) 759-1777

SAN DIEGO

A Black Mountain Road Pet Clinic
13161 Black Mountain Road, Suite 1
(858) 484-5000

ABC Veterinary Hospital of Kearny Mesa
8020 Ronson Road
(858) 278-1825

ABC Veterinary Hospital of Pacific Beach
2032 Hornblend Street
(858) 270-4120

All Care Cat Hospital
4680 Clairemont Mesa Boulevard
(858) 274-2287

American Animal Hospital
8135 Mira Mesa Boulevard, Suite 2
(858) 586-7387

Angel Animal Clinic of North Park
3537 30th Street
(619) 291-0042

Animal Center of San Diego
246 West Washington Street
(619) 299-7387

Animal Clinic of North Park
2444 University Avenue
(619) 295-1008

Animal Dermatology Clinic
5610 Kearny Mesa Road, Suite 2
(858) 560-9393

Animal Emergency Clinic
13240 Evening Creek Drive
(858) 748-7387

Animal ER of San Diego
5610 Kearny Mesa Road, Suite B
(858) 596-0600

Animal Eye Clinic of San Diego
2317 Hotel Circle South
(619) 293-7055

Animal Internal Medicine
5610 Kearny Mesa Road, Suite B
(858) 560-7778

Arena Animal Hospital
3625 Midway Drive
(619) 223-2166

Ark Animal Hospital
6171 Balboa Avenue
(858) 277-3665

Avian & Exotic Animal Hospital of San Diego
2317 Hotel Circle South
(619) 260-1412

Balboa Veterinary Hospital
7931 Balboa Avenue
(858) 279-0425

Bay Park Pet Clinic
1102 Morena Boulevard
(619) 276-1616

Bernardo Heights Veterinary
15721 Bernardo Heights Parkway
(858) 485-9111

Bird Rock Animal Clinic
5588 La Jolla Boulevard
(858) 459-3279

Black Mountain Road Pet Clinic
13161 Black Mountain Road
(858) 484-5000

Boulevard Animal Clinic
7047 El Cajon Boulevard
(619) 582-7250

If your dog is prone to hip dysplasia, keep him or her lean during the growing years. Extra weight ins not good for your dog's hip joints. Also, keep exercise light in order not to stress the joints. Ask your veterinarian for other tips and suggestions.

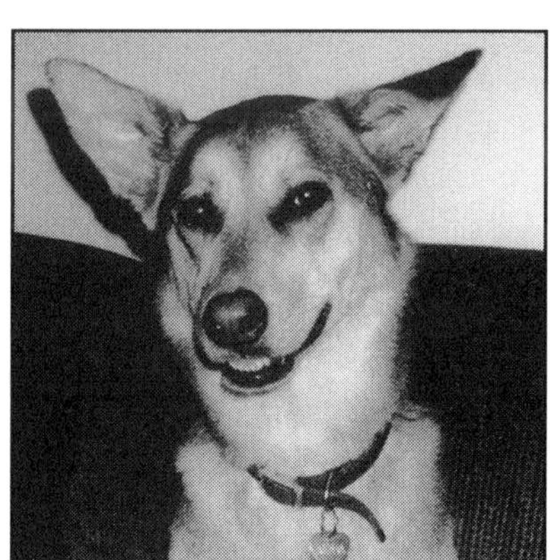

Always keep your veterinarian's and emergency clinic's phone number close at hand in case of an emergency. Post one on your refrigerator and keep one in your wallet or purse.

Cabrillo Veterinary Center
4138 Voltaire Street
(619) 225-9684

California Veterinary Neurosurgery/Surgical
2317 Hotel Circle South
(619) 299-5005

Carmel Mountain Ranch Veterinary
11925 Carmel Mountain Road
(858) 592-9779

Carmel Valley Pet Clinic
3890 Valley Centre Drive, Suite 101
(858) 259-8881

Center Veterinary Clinic
8963 Mira Mesa Boulevard
(858) 271-1152

Clairemont Rose Canyon Animal
4295 Jutland Drive
(858) 273-4680

Clairemont Square Animal Hospital
4941 Clairemont Drive
(858) 274-1760

Clairemont Village Pet Clinic
3007-G Clairemont Drive
(858) 275-5752

Colina Veterinary Hospital
5530 University Avenue
(619) 286-3360

College Animal Hospital
5653 El Cajon Boulevard
(619) 286-1980

Colony Veterinary Clinic
7748 Regents Road, Suite 302
(858) 450-5047

Companion Care Veterinary
16588 Bernardo Center Drive, #160
(858) 451-0990

Eye Clinic for Animals
2317 Hotel Circle South
(619) 293-7055

Friars Road Pet Hospital
10433 Friars Road, Suite E-F
(619) 282-7677

Genesee Bird & Pet Clinic
5621 Balboa Avenue
(858) 278-1575

Golden Triangle Veterinary Services
(858) 274-1760

Governor Animal Clinic
3218 Governor Drive
(858) 453-6312

Grand Animal Hospital
1033 Grand Avenue
(858) 272-1320

Grossmont Animal Hospital
(619) 466-0501

Hillcrest Veterinary Hospital
3949 1st Avenue
(619) 298-7714

Kearny Mesa Veterinary Center
7677 Ronson Road, Suite 100
(858) 279-3000

Kensington Veterinary Hospital
3817 Adams Avenue
(619) 584-8418

La Jolla Animal Hospital
7601 Draper Avenue
(858) 459-2665

La Jolla Veterinary Hospital
7520 Fay Avenue
(858) 454-6155

"A dry nose does not indicate a health problem with your dog. This is a wife's tale and has no basis in medical fact. A better way of diagnosing a sick pet would be to notice changes in behavior. A dog that is lethargic or not eating should be taken in for an examination."

Dr. John Hetzler, DVM
Ark Animal Hospital

If your dog is becoming overweight, evaluate your dog's diet and make changes appropriately. For instance, you may want to try feeding your dog smaller-portioned, lower-calorie meals more frequently throughout the day or avoid constant snacks and treats. Just as important, add an exercise program to your dog's daily routine, like regularly scheduled walks and increased play time.

Lifetime Animal Care Center
4941-G Clairemont Drive
(858) 274-1760

Main Street Small Animal Hospital
2773 Main Street
(619) 232-7401

Mira Mesa Veterinary Clinic
9396 Mira Mesa Boulevard
(858) 271-5515

Mission Gorge Animal Hospital
6690 Mission Gorge Road, Suite M
(858) 280-1503

Mission Valley Pet Clinic
4329 Twain Avenue
(858) 281-2934

Mobile Veterinary Service of San Diego
(619) 274-7005

Morena Pet Hospital & Bird Center
1540 Morena Boulevard
(858) 275-0888

Nautilus Vet Clinic of La Jolla
6911 La Jolla Boulevard
(858) 454-0354

North Park Veterinary Hospital
4054 Normal Street
(619) 299-6020

Northpark-Pacific Veterinary Clinic
2646 University Avenue
(619) 295-9025

Pacific Beach Veterinary Clinic
1362 Garnet Avenue
(858) 272-6255

Pacific PetCare
12720 Carmel Country Road, Suite 100
(858) 481-1101

Palm Ridge Pet Hospital
4370 Palm Avenue, Suite S
(619) 690-2272

Penasquitos Pet Clinic
9728 Carmel Mountain Road, Suite E
(858) 484-1260

Peninsula Veterinary Clinic
3767 Voltaire Street
(858) 223-7145

Pet Hospital of Penasquitos
9888 Carmel Mountain Road, Suite F
(858) 484-3490

Pet Hospital of Tierrasanta, The
6030 Santo Road, Suite A
(858) 569-7777

Point Loma Veterinary Clinic
2158 Catalina Boulevard
(619) 222-4482

Point Veterinary Clinic, The
140 Sylvester Road
(619) 224-3080

Rancho Bernardo Veterinary Clinic
12540 D Oaks North Road
(858) 487-4130

Rancho Mesa Animal Hospital
8710 Miramar Road
(858) 566-0422

Rancho San Carlos Pet Clinic
7850 Golfcrest Drive
(858) 462-6820

Renaissance Veterinary Clinic
8915 Towne Center Drive, Suite 110
(858) 452-7100

Rosecrans Pet Hospital
3786 Rosecrans Street
(619) 297-3857

There are many good books and guides on doggie health care. Check out your library or local bookstore for these books. Some Barnes & Noble bookstores even allow you to bring your well-behaved dog into the store.

"Symptoms of heat exhaustion include vomiting, diarrhea and lethargy. This is an emergency and you dog should be taken to the veterinarian immediately."

Dr. John Hetzler, DVM
Ark Animal Hospital

San Carlos Veterinary Hospital
8618 Lake Murray Boulevard
(619) 460-3100

Scripps Parkway Veterinary
10755 Scripps Poway Parkway
(858) 695-9996

Scripps Ranch Veterinary Hospital
9990 Scripps Ranch Boulevard
(858) 566-4912

Shelter Island Veterinary Clinic
1270 Scott Street
(619) 222-0597

South San Diego Veterinary
2910 Coronado Avenue
(619) 423-7121

Spay-Neuter Clinic
5530 University Avenue
(619) 286-3383

Sunset Cliffs Animal Clinic, Inc.
4741 Point Loma Avenue
(619) 224-0773

Tierramesa Veterinary Clinic
9353-Q Clairemont Mesa Boulevard
(858) 268-0044

Tierrasanta Veterinary Hospital
10799 Tierrasanta Boulevard
(858) 292-6116

Turquoise Animal Hospital
950 Turquoise Street
(858) 488-0658

University City Veterinary Clinic
3961 Governor Drive
(858) 453-6757

University City Veterinary Services
3218 Governor Drive
(858) 453-6312

VCA Emergency Animal Hospital
2317 Hotel Circle South
(619) 299-2400

VCA Hillcrest Animal Center
246 W. Washington Street
(619) 299-7387

Vetco Animal Hospital
3994 Clairemont Mesa Boulevard
(858) 483-4145

Veterinary House Call Service
2646 University Avenue
(619) 295-9025

Veterinary Surgical Specialists
5610 Kearny Mesa Road, Suite B
(858) 560-8006

Vetsmart Veterinary Hospital
3396 Murphy Canyon Road
(858) 565-9780

Westwood Bernardo Veterinary
11605 Duenda Road, Suite D
(858) 485-7570

SAN MARCOS

ABC Veterinary Hospital of San
330 Rancheros Drive
(760) 471-4950

California Veterinary Specialists
100 N. Rancho Santa Fe Road
(760) 734-4433

Levitt Animal Hospital
1155 Grand Avenue
(760) 744-5242

Mohnacky Animal Hospital
997 W. San Marcos Boulevard
(760) 744-0032

If your dog gets into a fight with another dog and your dog's ear gets bitten or lacerated, take him or her to the veterinarian right away. He or she may need stitches to prevent curling of the ear or even cosmetic surgery to reconstruct the ear.

Pet prescriptions can cost a lot of money if you are buying them directly from your veterinarian or veterinary hospital. Check with your local pharmacist to see if they can fill your dog's prescription. Many prescriptions for your dog are the same medicine used for humans. And don't forget to ask for generics!

North County Emergency Animal
100 B Rancho Santa Fe Road, Suite 133
(760) 734-4433

Palomar Animal Hospital
2615 South Santa Fe
(760) 727-7622

Pearson's Animal Hospital
1903 W. San Marcos Boulevard
(760) 598-2512

San Marcos Veterinary Clinic
145 S. Rancho Santa Fe Road
(760) 744-5400

SANTEE

Mast Boulevard Pet Care Center
9740 Magnolia Avenue
(619) 448-6490

Santee Pet Hospital
8936 Carlton Hills Boulevard
(619) 449-4100

SOLANA BEACH

ABC Veterinary Hospital of Solana
140 S. Solana Hills Drive
(858) 350-6353

Academy Animal Hospital
741 Academy Drive
(858) 755-1511

SPRING VALLEY

Paradise Valley Road Pet Hospital
8360 Paradise Valley Road
(619) 475-9770

Spring Valley Veterinary Clinic
9973 Campo Road
(619) 660-1114

VISTA

A Coastal Emergency Animal
1900 Hacienda Drive
(760) 630-6343

Alta Mira Animal Hospital
998 S. Santa Fe Avenue
(760) 726-8918

Animal Imaging & Treatment Center
1925 West Vista Way
(760) 726-7014

Booman House Call Veterinary
2302 Bautista Avenue
(760) 630-2250

Brengle Terrace Animal Hospital
971 Vale Terrace Drive
(760) 724-7186

Melrose Veterinary Hospital
1680 S. Melrose Drive
(760) 727-5151

Shadow Ridge VLG Veterinary
751 Shadow Ridge Road
(760) 727-7900

Tri-City Veterinary Clinic
1929 W. Vista Way
(760) 758-2091

Vetsmart Veterinary Hospital
1740 University Drive
(760) 414-1530

Vista Veterinary Hospital
1139 S. Santa Fe Avenue
(760) 726-1234

If your dog's eyes are starting to fail, there are things you can do to make life a little easier while your dog is adapting:

- *Keep things where your dog will remember where they are such as his food and dog bowls.*
- *Doggie proof unsafe areas such as putting up a child's gate at the edge of the stairs.*
- *Strengthen your dog's other senses by taking your dog outdoors to explore new smells, buying squeaky toys for hearing and petting or playfully wrestling with your dog for touch.*

NOTES

Chapter Ten

©Casey Orr

Training

Training

The goal of dog training is first and foremost to create a loving bond between owner and animal. All the rest - a well-behaved, socialized animal you can take anywhere - is gravy compared with the trust that is gained by training with your pet.

©Casey Orr

Obedience training means training a dog to obey everything they are told to do. Depending on your skill and dedication, these lessons can range from teaching cute tricks and simple family manners, to show ring exercises, to the skills necessary becoming highly trained service dogs. Some breeds will also enjoy agility training, in which a dog is given a set amount of time to go through an obstacle course off-leash.

Most dog owners simply want their dogs to be well-mannered and to respond to basic commands. Whatever type of training you decide to pursue, it should start early. A puppy should be socialized to people and taken wherever he can. By eight weeks he should be able to sit on command and walk on a leash. By 20 weeks, your dog's lifelong social tendencies are set. Although you can teach an old dog new tricks, it's much easier to start early and begin the process correctly.

So, how to start? In the next chapter, we'll list the various trainers available in our area. We'll also provide you with pointers and quotes about dog training.

Training your dog properly will make your dog happy and easy to care for, but will also enhance your relationship. Ultimately, you'll end up with a well-behaved animal that is a joy to be around.

CARLSBAD

Affection Dog Training
(760) 476-9413

Canine Learning Centers
P.O. Box 2010
(760) 931-1834
www.K9LRNG.com

Canines Content
7113 Manzanita Drive
(760) 929-9252

Pacific Coast K-9's Seacrest
7250 Ponto Drive
(760) 438-2469

Spoke N Paw
2131 Palomar Airport Road
(760) 602-5222

CHULA VISTA

Bahia Sur Kennel Club of Chula Vista
(619) 420-8404

EAST COUNTY

Cape-Able Canine
(619) 589-7510

EL CAJON

Canine Sports Center
4821 Dehesa Road
(619) 588-4821

Petsmart
865 Jackman Street
(619) 442-0600

ENCINITAS

Animal Keeper The
155 Saxony Road
(760) 753-9366
www.animalkeeper.com

©Casey Orr

"Formal obedience training should take place after the 8th week of life. Lifelong social tendencies for dogs are set between 8 and 20 weeks of age, so it's important to get them on the right path early."

Dr. John Hetzler, DVM
Ark Animal Hospital

Look for these things when shopping for a trainer:

- *Excellent references.*
- *Experience.*
- *Humane training methods.*
- *Dog behavioral knowledge.*
- *Devotion to dogs.*
- *Good communication skills.*
- *Affiliations to reputable associations.*
- *Good sense of humor.*
- *Good ethics.*

John's Natural Dog Training
1985 Olivenhain Road
(760) 737-6100
www.johnknowsdogs.com

Lu Meyer's Obedience Academy
464 Cole Ranch Road
(760) 436-3571

North Coast Dog Training
1985 Olivenhain Road
(760) 753-5203

ESCONDIDO

Chosen Dog The
(619) 749-4235

Hidden Valley Obedience Club
(858) 259-5307

Nordhein Police K-9 Institute
1863 Golden Circle Drive
(760) 741-3390

Super Puppy Press
(800) 342-7877
www.superpuppy.com

LA MESA

A Better Canine School for Dogs
7330 University Avenue
(619) 465-5630

ABC School for Dogs
7330 University Avenue
(619) 466-1877
www.ABCDogTrainingTruths.com

LAKE FOREST

Welsh & Associates Canine Training
24412 Muirlands Boulevard
(760) 723-2166

NORTH COUNTY

Canine Learning Centers
(760) 931-1834
www.k9lrng.com

A Dog's Life
(760) 745-6621

Absolute K9 Training
(800) 889-3647

Chosen Dog Agility
(760) 749-4235

Copilots for Independence Service
(760) 734-0065
www.copilots.org

Dog Training Scooby's Way
(760) 751-9171

Dog Training with Liz
(760) 630-4824

Dogworks
(858) 513-0364

Doggie Tech
(760) 745-1011

Great Dogs Training & Education
(858) 679-7538

John's Natural Dog Training Service
(760) 737-6100

Nancy Weiss Training & Care
(760) 752-8682

Pacific Coast K-9 Services
(800) 598-7246

Pro-Train
(877) 223-3647
www.protraindog.com

Humane training include methods that train your dog in an effective yet gentle manner, using positive, motivational reinforcement.

©Casey Orr

"Once you let your dogs train you, you'll be much happier!"

Karen Campos
Max - German shepherd/ greyhound mix
La Mesa

©Casey Orr

San Pasqual Stock Dog Training
(760) 739-8673

Super Puppy
(760) 489-6775

Uncommon Canine
(858) 679-5861

OCEANSIDE

Animal Keeper The
3532 College Boulevard
(760) 941-3221
www.animalkeeper.com

Canine Companions for
124 Rancho Del Oro Drive
(760) 754-3300

Oceanside Pet Hotel & Training
2909 San Luis Rey Road
(760) 757-2345
www.go.to/OPH

POWAY

Good Dog Training Center
(619) 748-7943

RANCHO SANTA FE

Animals First
(858) 756-5545

University of California Veterinary
6525 Calle Del Nido
(858) 759-6837

SAN DIEGO

Absoulute K9 Training
(800) 889-3647

Academy of Canine Trainers
(619) 447-1831

All Breed Obedience Club, Inc.
(619) 287-2211

American Canine Training
(858) 274-0268
www.sdnet.com/americancanine.html

Behaviorist & Dog Training, Matthew Perry
(619) 596-6832

Best Friend Puppy Classes
(619) 460-3647

Best Friends Pet Resort & Salon
8020 Ronson Road
(858) 565-8055

Camera One Canine Training
(619) 688-1043

Cape-Able Canines
(619) 697-7383

D Squared Dog Training
(619) 225-2251

Dogworks
(858) 513-0364
www.dgwrks.com

Dr. Dog
(858) 485-7433

Dream Dogs
(619) 445-9788

Educated Pet The
(619) 466-5098

Enjoy Your Dog Training School
7933 Balboa Avenue
(858) 467-1409
www.enjoyyourdog.com

Euro Dog Training
(800) 968-7677

Fon Jon Kennels
5050 Santa Fe Street
(858) 273-2266

©Casey Orr

Dogs can get bored. Try to keep training fun for both you and your dog in order to keep interest high. Break up training sessions by playing fetch or playfully wrestling with your dog.

"If you do not want your dog to jump on you when you come home from work, then you should never allow your dog to jump on you. You will confuse your dog if you allow them to greet you by jumping up on you sometimes and at other times, yelling, "No!" Always be consistent."

Jorge Mendoza
Bear - Chow Chow
North Park

German Shepherd Dog Club of San Diego
(858) 560-1332

Hankins Family Dog Training
(619) 225-9176

Hawaiiana Canine School
(619) 443-7780

Joanne Griffin
(619) 276-1925

Markim Pet Resort
(858) 481-3881

Obedience Club of San Diego
(619) 273-5034

Personal K-9 Training
(619) 295-7203

Petsmart
3396 Murphy Canyon Road
(858) 571-0300

Petsmart
3610 Rosecrans
(619) 523-4177

Proper Pup
(619) 390-0644

San Diego Dog
(858) 546-7831

San Diego Humane Society
887 Sherman
(619) 299-7012

SD Hunter Retriever Club
(858) 459-6614

South Bark Dog Wash
2037 30th Street
(619) 232-7387

Special Care, Cindy Binno
(619) 585-9247

Superdog Dog Training
(858) 547-8323

Top Dog Obedience Training
(858) 449-7651

Wilson Lynn, PhD.
(619) 281-6067

SAN MARCOS

All Things Canine
P.O. Box 1719
(760) 471-7444

Paw-Dre's Clubhouse for Pets
1049 E. Mission Road
(760) 745-2759

San Marcos Training & Boarding
130 S. Twin Oaks Valley Road
(760) 744-5171

SPRING VALLEY

Ball Park
3971 Spring Drive
(619) 461-5577

Jay Bee's Kennels
9124 Olive Drive
(619) 463-0207

VISTA

Country Feed Store
2111 E. Vista Way
(760) 724-7310

Country Feed Store The
2111 E. Vista Way
(760) 724-7310

©Casey Orr

"Don't nag... it doesn't work for people, it won't work for your dog. Give a command only once, gently make your dog to perform that command and then praise or reward him right afterwards."

Martin Rivera
Pastor Aleman -
German shepherd
City Heights

NOTES

Chapter Eleven

Clubs & Special Events

Clubs & Special Events

©Casey Orr

San Diego is full of special events designed for you and your dog. Whether it's a health-related seminar, agility competitions, a dog show, a walk for charity, or a contest featuring the ugliest dog in the city - you are sure to find something entertaining year-round.

Are you interested in a particular breed? Many clubs have educational seminars, health clinics, conformation shows, and obedience trials for your favorite breed. We'll let you know what breeds have local clubs and where they meet.

Would you like your dog to become involved in a particular sport? San Diego has herding events, agility training, obedience trials and other dog-related sporting events year round. We'll tell you where they meet and how to find them.

Dog shows attract dog lovers and professional breeders alike. Watch your favorite compete and perhaps be judged Best in Show! There are many annual dog shows in San Diego, and if you love dogs, these shows are the place to be. Not only will you see the various breeds in action, but you can also check out the latest in dog foods and accessories.

Fund-raising events are also a great source of fun, and a good place to put your money. Many events take place throughout the year and range from wacky to the sedate, and raise money for all sorts of charities, most of them dog-related. The annual ones will be listed in the coming pages.

There is a wide variety of events in San Diego, and we have listed as many of them as we can. There are new ones cropping up each month however, so keep your eyes open.

Clubs

Australian Shepherd Club of San Diego
(619) 670-7249

Belgian Tervuren Club of Southern California
(818) 899-3407

Boxer Club of Southern California
(909) 657-3906

Bulldog Club of San Diego
(619) 447-9711

Del Dios Shetland Sheepdog Club
(619) 561-6085

Golden Retriever Club of San Diego
(619) 436-1481

Keeshond Club of Southern California
(714) 780-1522

San Diego Cocker Spaniel Club
(619) 789-1389

San Diego Dachshund Club
(619) 274-3655

San Diego German Shepherd Club
(619) 560-1332

San Diego Lhasa Apso Club
(619) 789-4864

San Diego Poodle Club
(619) 724-9134

Sport Clubs

Aztec Schutzhund Club
(619) 674-1436

©Casey Orr

The benefits of joining a club are many. You can learn about a particular breed of dog and in turn educate others about the breed, socialize, get exercise for you and your dog and have fun.

When driving into an event, drive slowly. You never know when one of your fellow four-legged friends may jump out of nowhere.

Blazin' Border Collies
(619) 739-8673
Herding training. All breeds.

Catchers on the Fly
(619) 630-1723
Hidden Valley Obedience Club's Flyball Team.

Herding Breed Club of San Diego
(858) 748-2111
Herding.

Lickety Splits
(858) 729-1977
Aztec Doberman Pinscher Club's Flyball Team. All dogs welcome.

North County Schutzhund Club
(858) 726-3684

Special Events

Contact these organizations directly to get on their mailing lists and to find out specific dates and time for their upcoming events.

Annual Pug Party
(619) 299-3580
Presented by Pug Rescue

Annual Kiwanis St. Patrick's Day Ugly Dog Contest
(858) 755-5913
Del Mar Fairgrounds
Sponsored by the Del Mar Kiwanis in March at the Del Mar Fairgrounds. It benefits the Rancho Coastal Humane Society Safehouse Program, Helen Woodward Therapeutic Riding Program and Canine Companion for Independence.

Annual Walk & Roll for Independence
(760) 754-3300
www.miracosta.cc.ca.us/home/charr
Benefits Canine Companions for Independence.

Bahia Sur Kennel Club All-breed AKC Show
(619) 542-0540

Bowling for the Animals
9528 Miramar Road, PMB 160, San Diego
Benefits the Escondido Humane Society & Center for Humane Education, Wild Burro Rescue, the Feral Cat Coalition and San Diego Animal Advocates.

Cape-able Canines
(619) 697-7383

Chula Vista Animal Shelter Pet Parade & Pageant
(619) 421-3111
www.eastlake.net

Dog Beach Cleanup
Ocean Beach Dog Beach
(619) 523-1700
Sponsored by Friends of Dog Beach and Dog Beach Dog Wash in honor of Earth Day. Provisions include: gloves, bags, scoops, brooms, shovels plus toys & treats for you and your dog.

Escondido Humane Society Events
(760) 745-4362

F.O.C.A.S.
(619) 685-3536

Front Runners San Diego Dog Days of Summer Fun Run
www.frsd.org/events/events.htm
Event includes fun run/walk, "Dog Gone" prizes, tricks for doggies and treats people.

Helen Woodward Animal Center
(858) 756-4117
www.AnimalCenter.org
The center offers wide-variety of events hosted throughout the year. Consult their website or call them for further information.

When going to an event:

- *Keep your dog on the leash.*
- *Bring shade for your dog – it may be hot.*
- *Keep an eye on your dog and hang out under the trees once in awhile to the keep them cool.*
- *Bring water.*

©Casey Orr

For additional information on upcoming events or changes, call the clubs, humane organizations or shelters for updates. Also check out Thursday's Union Tribune "Animal House" Section for everyday events.

Molly's Annual Halloween Party
14845 Pomerado Road
(858) 679-7967
Sponsored by Molly's Gourmet Bakery & Gifts. Costume contest, free "Goodies Bag" for dogs in costume and agility/obstacle course.

North County Humane Society
(760) 757-4357
The center offers wide-variety of events hosted throughout the year.

Rancho Coastal Humane Society
(760) 753-6413
The center offers wide-variety of events hosted throughout the year.

San Diego Humane Society & SPCA
(619) 299-7012
www.sdhumane.org
The center offers wide-variety of events hosted throughout the year. Consult their website or call them for further information.

Woofstock
P.O. Box 2433
La Mesa, CA 91943
(619) 443-0940
Benefits the Greyhound Adoption Center

Silver Bay Kennel Club
Soft-Coated Wheaten Terrier Club of So. Calif
(310) 947-1770

Southern California Airedale Terrier Club
(818) 506-0961

Southern California Beagle Club
(714) 826-0928

Southern California Scottish Terrier Club
(818) 353-0657

Southwestern Rottweiler Club of San Diego
(619) 645-8800

NOTES

NOTES

Chapter Twelve

Humane Societies, Rescues & Humanitarian Organizations

Humane Societies, Rescues & Humanitarian Organizations

As dog lovers, we are deeply committed to the concept of the humane treatment of our canine companions. Dogs add value and love to our lives, and we believe that they should be always treated compassionately and responsibly. To that end, we are listing humane organizations within the county that are also committed to that goal. We feel that it's important to let you, as a pet owner, know what resources are there for you in a time of need.

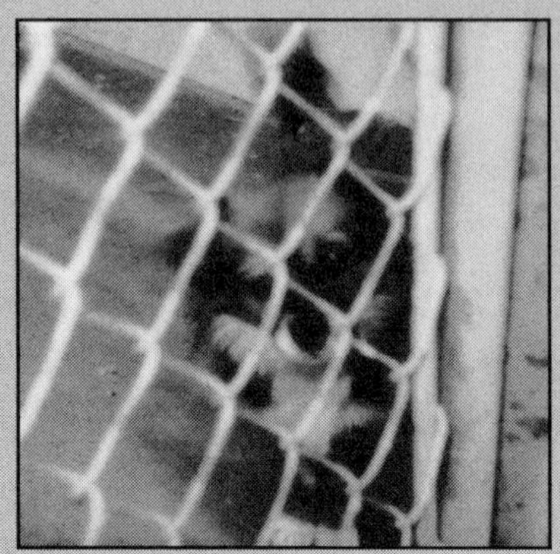

Adoption: *Adopting a puppy is easy - they are adorable and sweet. However, it takes a special person to adopt an older dog. There are many advantages to doing so, among them getting to choose the personality of your pet in advance. These adult dogs can be particularly grateful and give you years of loving companionship. Shelters are good places to find your new pet, and many retail stores offer adoption services. Pet adoptions happen every weekend all over the city.*

Dog Rescues: *Dog Rescues are non-profit referral organizations that place unwanted dogs in homes, bypassing the shelter system. Many of these organizations focus on a particular breed. We'll list them and tell you how to find a dog or contribute to your favorite charity.*

Humane Organizations: *Under this heading we'll list groups designed to help the animal population in various ways. Groups such as PETA are well-known for their desire to protect our animal friends, but there are numerous other groups which focus on caring for the dog population. Some specialize in attending to the elderly dog, and some are no-kill shelters that care for the unwanted pet population.*

The humane treatment of animals along with responsible pet ownership can enrich the lives of both animal and owner. The help and education necessary to create a good life for your dog is readily available and you'll find great information in this chapter.

Humane Societies & Shelters

Camp Pendleton Animal Shelter
Area 25 Vado Del Rio, Building 25132
(760) 725-8120

Central County Shelter
5480 Gaines Street, San Diego
(619) 236-4250
www.sddac.com
PetLink 24-hours: (619) 294-2063
for automated information about lost/found pets and adoption pets. Contact them for volunteer opportunities.

City Of Chula Vista
130 Byer Road
(619) 691-5123
Chula Vista, Imperial Beach & National City

City of Coronado
1015 65th Street
(619) 522-7371

City of El Cajon Shelter
1275 N. Marshall Avenue
(619) 441-1580
El Cajon & La Mesa

Escondido Humane Society
P.O. Box 460249
(760) 839-0293
www.escondidohumanesociety.org

FOCAS- Friends of County Animal Shelters-Adoption
(619) 685-3536
www.focas-sandiego.org
Adoption of County Shelter Pets

www.papillonclub.org/rescue

"If you lose your dog, call every humane society and animal shelter around. Then visit them to see if your dog is there. When Benito ran away, we called the local shelters and they said there was no such dog in their kennels. I decided to check out the shelters with my daughter just to make sure, and sure enough, Benito was there."

Afshin Oskoui
Benito - Pomeranian
La Mesa

www.papillonclub.org/rescue

"If there's a particular breed of dog that you really want, check out all your humane societies and animal shelters. Also, there are breed rescues all over the country for most every breed of dog. It's better to rescue a dog in need of a home and love than buying one from a store or breeder whose main purpose is profit."

Helen Woodward Animal Care & Education Center
6461 El Apajo Road
(858) 756-4117
www.animalcenter.org

North County Humane Society & SPCA
2905 San Luis Rey Road
(760) 757-4357
www.nchumane.org
Independent organization focused on adopting out animals, responding to cruelty calls, animals running loose.

North County Shelter
2481 Palomar Airport Road
(760) 438-2312
www.sddac.com
PetLink 24-hours: (619) 294-2063 for automated information about lost/found pets and adoption pets.

Rancho Coastal Humane Society
389 Requeza Street
(760) 753-6413
www.rchumanesociety.org
Accept owner relinquished dogs, and some from animal control but no strays. They keep dogs until they are adopted. Second chance program.

San Diego Humane Society & SPCA
887 Sherman Street
(619) 299-7012
No strays.

South Country Shelter
5821 Sweetwater Road
(619) 263-7741
www.sddac.com
PetLink 24-hours: (619) 294-2063 for automated information about lost/found pets and adoption pets.

www.AdoptMe2000.com
This web site is dedicated to assisting animals up for adoption in the San Diego area.

Breed Rescues

Afghan Hound Rescue
(213) 427-9667

Akita Support and Placement
917 W. 17th Street
Santa Ana, CA 92706
(800) 392-8414

Alaskan Malamute Rescue of California
(805) 583-8250

All Retriever Friends (ARF)
(866) 462-2773
www.arfdogs.com/arrfinc

American Eskimo Rescue
(858) 452-7496

Basenji Rescue
(818) 761-7668

Basset Hound Rescue & Adoption, Inc
(619) 286-8638

Beagles and Buddies
(626) 444-9664

Begian Malinois Rescue
(818) 558-7560

Benevolent Animal Rescue Committee
(909) 696-2428

Boxer Rescue and Referral
(760) 747-5712

Bulldog Club of Greater San Diego
(619) 685-8582

Cairn Terrier Rescue
(760) 728-7133

California Breed Rescues
www.rescuers.com

"My dogs are my entertainment, my recreation and my therapy - all at he same time. Does that make them therapy dogs?"

Carol Drummond
Boomer and Blizzard - Great Pyrenees
Chance - Australian Shepherd
Lakeside

Get your kids interested in volunteering at your local shelter or humane organization. They can learn something new, help animals, feel good about themselves and stay out of trouble. There are many programs for kids that suit different interests. Call your shelter or a humane organization for available programs.

Chines Crested
Fontana, CA
(909) 829-4744
www.geocities.com/ccclubsc

Collie Rescue, Southland
(626) 398-8987
www.collie.org

Dachshund Rescue of San Diego
(858) 560-4022
www.DachshundRescue.org

English Springer Spaniel Rescue
(309) 276-5525

German Shepherd Rescue
(818) 558-7560

German Shepherd Rescue
(858) 576-1016

German Shorthair Pointer Rescue
(760) 726-4813

Golden Retriever Rescue
(619) 445-9216

Great Pyrenees Association of So. Calif.
(909) 887-8201
www.greatpyrrescue.org

Greyhound Connection
(619) 286-4739

Greyhound Adoption Center
(619) 443-0940

Irish Wolfhound Rescue Trust
(818) 894-8988

Italian Greyhound Rescue
(909) 829-4744

Papillon Club
www.papillonclub.org/rescue
See adorable dogs presently in foster care waiting to be adopted. Applications for adoption on line.

Pug Rescue of San Diego County
P.O. Box 151449
San Diego, CA 92175-1449
(619) 685-3580

Rescue House The
132 N. El Camino Real, #292
Encinitas, CA 92024
(760) 591-1211
www.rescuehouse.org

Retriever Rescue & BARC
P.O. Box 151449
San Diego, CA 92175-1449
(909) 696-2428
www.rescuers.com/BARC

Rottweiler Rescue
(619) 460-7555

Samoyed Rescue
(714) 956-6180

San Diego Poodle Club
(760) 758-7322

Scottie Rescue
(714) 893-5821

Shiba Inu Rescue
(858) 452-7496

Siberian Husky Rescue of San Diego
San Diego
(760) 744-7694

Southwestern Rottweiler Club of San Diego Rescue
San Diego
(619) 645-8800

"Dogs are like a real friend and your real friends you can talk to, and be confident that they will never pass judgement."

Joaquin Rivera
Tio - Labrador
City Heights

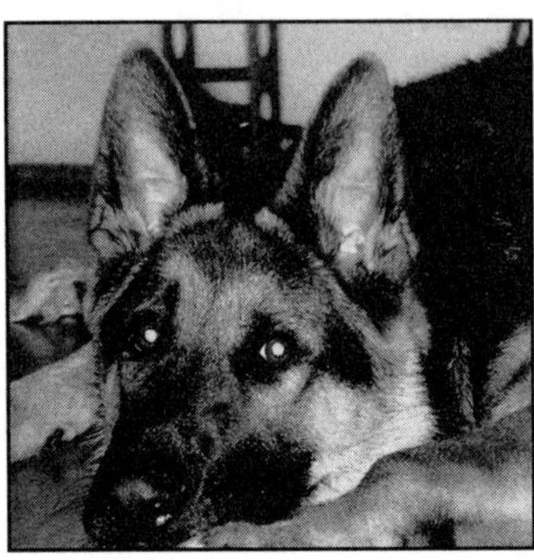

Before adopting a dog, evaluate the following things:

- *Do you have time to take care of a new family member?*
- *Is there adequate, safe space for a dog?*
- *Do you have enough money for pet food and veterinary bills?*
- *If you have other pets, will they get along with another pet?*
- *Do all other family members want a pet?*

Humanitarian Organizations

AniMeals - Helen Woodward Animal Center
6461 El Apajo Road
(858) 756-4117
www.animalcenter.org

Canine Companions for Independence
(760) 754-3300
Volunteers needed to raise puppies, work in kennels and groom.

Cars for Critters - Helen Woodward Animal Center
6461 El Apajo Road
(858) 756-4117
www.animalcenter.org
Donate your car for support the Helen Woodward Animal Center. Cars do not have to run and free towing is offered. They accept cars, boats, and RV's.

FOCAS- Friends of County Animal Shelters-Adoption
(619) 685-3536
www.focas-sandiego.org

Adoption of County Shelter Pets
Foundation for the Care of Indigent Animals
(619) 466-9137

Helen Woodward Animal Center
6461 El Apajo Road
(858) 756-4117
www.animalcenter.org

Last Chance for Animals - Animal Rights Group
(619) 583-9522

Mercy Crusade of San Diego Inc.
(858) 278-1745
Assists seniors, low income and disabled persons to pay vet bills. Volunteers needed.

PAWS (Pets Are Wonderful Support) - North County
(760) 743-8233
www.nctimes.net/~pawsnc/index.htm
Free pet information and rescue referral.

People for the Ethical Treatment of Animals (PETA)
www.peta-online.org

Pet Encounter Therapy (P.E.T.) - Helen Woodward Animal Center
6461 El Apajo Road
(858) 756-4117
www.animalcenter.org

San Diego Animal Advocates (SDAA)
(760) 943-0330
www.AnimalAdvocates.org
An all-volunteer, non-profit animal rights organization founded in 1984.

San Diego Animal Rescue
P.O. Box 1604
(619) 390-7585

San Diego Animal Shelters Foundation
1150 Silverado Road
(858) 551-8474

Buddy

Ode to Buddy

Small and furry as if he were
Winston
The day we got him,
Now, big and fat like a pig.
He roams the neighborhood
In search of something to do.
Once a fluffy marshmallow,
Now roasted gold.
Either incessantly chewing his
bone,
Or laying on my mother's feet,
He always can find a way to
get in the way.
With his whale-like nose
He can send chills up your
spine
By thrusting his cold, wet nose
between your toes.
Although sometimes smelling
like soap,
He usually reeks beyond words.
Young or old, he always feels
soft as silk.
I will always remember him
Laying down, wagging his tail,
and salivating
As he does everyday after his
run.
He barks and yelps for my
attention.
Too bad he doesn't know he'll
always have it!

Lauren Henry
Buddy - Yellow Lab
Chula Vista

NOTES

Chapter Thirteen

Artists & Photographers

Artists & Photographers

Your dog is part of your family, and what is more important to family history than having a portrait taken? Memorializing the ones we love is human nature, and a good photograph or painting of your dog will be cherished for years to come.

When you decide to find a photographer or artist to capture your pup, you'll have to think in advance what kind of portrait you want. Some photographers specialize in catching your pet in action. If you have a show dog, an agility-trained dog, or a pet that adores chasing balls in the park, an action photographer may be the one for you. If, however, your pooch likes nothing better than reclining on the couch getting his ears scratched, a studio photograph might be the best choice.

If you choose to have an artist rendition of your pet, the cost will be typically be a bit more than a photograph, and you'll need to think in advance about the medium: do you want a charcoal drawing, an oil painting, or a watercolor? Most artists will work from a photograph of your pet, so you'll need to provide a clear one with the details you hope to remember.

Choosing an artist or photographer will take a bit of research. You'll want to see examples of their work first and, of course, compare prices. You'll decide whether you want to be in the picture, where you want it shot, and which characteristics of your dog you wish to feature.

Having a professional depiction of your special companion will add timeless memories to your life. San Diego has some excellent animal portrait artists and we'll list them in this next chapter.

A Picture Perfect Mobile Pet Grooming & Photography
(760) 787-1555
Photography

Eleanor Becher
(619) 464-1798
Artist

Pat Beck
(619) 942-1907
Artist

Rich Bergman
(619) 443-5688
Photography

Camera One Canine Actors
(619) 688-1043
Photography

Everyday Moments/Graphic Details
(858) 581-6007
www.everydaymoments.com
www.gdetails.com
Greeting cards/calendars created from your favorite canine photos.

Meredith French
(619) 260-1588
Photography

Karryn Photography
(800) 773-8749
Photography

Marie Staddon Designs/Photography
(310) 798-0791
www.poundpets.com
Pound Pets (Greeting Cards of rescued animals - 5% of proceeds go to shelter.
Photography

To take a really good picture of your dog, make sure nothing surrounds your dog so he or she isn't competing with clutter in your photo.

Somehow, dogs know when you are going to take their picture and tend to get bored easily. So, fix up the area you want to take your dog's picture without creating too much fuss. Then take your picture. Usually the first photo will be the best.

©Casey Orr

Murals and Portraits
(760) 789-5412
Photography

My Beautiful Dog-O-Mat
(619) 295-6140
Photography

Pair-A-Docs Fine Art
(858) 259-0561
Photography

Pet Pixs
(800) 773-8749
Photography

Picture Perfect International
(619) 281-4829
www.PicturePerfectInternational.com
Photography

Pam Posey
(619) 724-3599
Artist

Laura Rogers
(619) 345-0062
Artist

Shadow Catcher Creations
(760) 941-5041
Water Colors, Pencil Photography
Photography

Sinclair Stratton - Fine Artist Pet Portrait
(800) 824-2272
www.sinclairstratton.com
Artist

The Blend Magazine Pet Portraits
(760) 941-5041
www.theblendmagazine.com/artreid
Photography

NOTES

NOTES

Chapter Fourteen

Bereavement

Bereavement

Nobody wants to think about the loss of a beloved pet, yet it's something we all must eventually face. Those who have lost a dog know the heartache and pain this experience can cause. Society does not always support the feelings of anguish that arise from a dog's demise, and this lack of support can further exacerbate the feelings of loneliness and grief.

Fortunately, there are compassionate organizations in San Diego dedicated to helping people during this special type of grief. Some organizations offer support groups that allow you to discuss your feelings of loss in the safety of others who are experiencing the same thing. Others provide individual counseling sessions with professional psychologists. If you are faced with a very ill pet and are contemplating euthanasia, there are also specialized groups that can help you make this very difficult decision.

One of the most vital steps in coping with the emotions you will feel upon the loss of your pet is acknowledging them. Some of the resources listed on the next pages are available to help you through this process. Through them, you will realize that the grief, depression and guilt you may feel upon the loss of your beloved friend is perfectly natural and that eventually, while you'll never forget the love you shared, time will eventually heal the pain.

Counseling

Lorri A. Green, Ph. D.
Pet Loss Counseling
4295 Gesner Street, San Diego
(619) 275-0728

Ryan Kenneth, Ph. D.
Pet Loss Counseling
4295 Gesner Street, San Diego
(619) 275-0728

PetFriends
Bereavement Support Hotline
(800) 404-PETS

Pet Loss Support Hotline
University of California, Davis
(916) 752-4200

The Rainbow Passage
Support for people dealing with animal illness or death.
http://members.tripod.com/~phildogs/rainbow/rainbow.htm

Cemeteries & Crematorians

San Diego Pet Memorial Park
8995 Crestmar Point
(858) 271-4242
www.sandiegopetmemorial.com

Sorrento Valley Pet Cemetery & Crematory
10801 Sorrento Valley Road
(619) 276-3361

©Casey Orr

Letting go will be the most difficult thing you will have to do when it comes to your best friend. Unfortunately, your companion is depending on you to make that decision. Keep his or her best interest in mind and evaluate dignity, pain and quality of life. You can ask your veterinarian to assist you with your decision and to provide different options.

If you and your veterinarian have decided that its time, you may consider having your vet euthanize your beloved pet at home, making his or her passing peaceful and dignified.

Virtual Cemeteries

In Memory of Pets
www.in-memory-of-pets.com

NetKin's Dog Heaven
www.netkin.com/creatures/home.php3

O'Petuaries
www.angelfire.com/ab2/opets/index.html

Pawprints in Heaven
www.pawprintsinheaven.com

Pet Garden
www.petgarden.com

Virtual Pet Cemetery
www.mycemetery.com

Books for Children

Death of a Pet – Answers to Questions for Children Animal Lovers of all Ages
By J. W. Potter
(Guideline Publications)
(800) 552-1076

"Oh, Where Has My Pet Gone?"
A Pet Loss Memory Book
By Sally Sibbitt
(Libby Press)

The Tenth Good Thing About Barney
By Judith Viorst
(Macmillan)

Other References

SuperDog Pet Dog Training
www.superdog.com/petloss.htm

NOTES

NOTES

Jane's Dog Guide

1010 Second Avenue, Suite 150B, Box 22, San Diego, CA 92101
619-280-7699 • 619-280-7596 fax • www.janesdogguide.com

ORDER FORM

Bill to/Ship to: (No P.O. Boxes)

Name: ____________________

Address: ____________________

City: ____________________

State: ________ Postal/Zip: ____________________

Phone: ____________________

Fax: ____________________

E-Mail: ____________________

URL: ____________________

Delivery/Special Instructions: ____________________

____

Description	Quantity	Price
***Jane's Dog Guide* to San Diego**		***$14.95 each***
Shipping - $3.50 per order	TOTAL	
20% discount for orders of 10 or more books	Shipping	
	CA Sales tax (7.5%)	
	GRAND TOTAL	

Payment Method

☐ Check ☐ Money Order ☐ VISA ☐ MasterCard ☐ American Express

Expiration: ☐☐/☐☐

Card No: ☐☐☐☐ ☐☐☐☐ ☐☐☐☐ ☐☐☐☐

Name on Card: ____________________

Signature: ____________________

TO ORDER COPIES OF THIS BOOK, CALL:
619-280-7699
OR COMPLETE THIS FORM AND FAX IT TO:
619-280-7596
OR EMAIL US AT: JANESDOGGUIDE@HOME.COM

NOTES

NOTES

NOTES

NOTES

NOTES

NOTES

NOTES